KB166839

EVERYDAY K-LINGO

EVERYDAY K-LINGO

Written by Cho Jae-hee, Kim Doe-hee, Sohn Jung-ran
Translated by Katelyn Hemmeke
First Published March, 2024
First Printing April, 2024
Publisher Chung Kyudo
Editor Lee Suk-hee, Baek Da-heuin, Lee Hyeon-soo
Cover design your-txt
Interior design your-txt
Illustrated by Yoon Byung-chul
Voice Actor Kim Rae-whan, Shin So-yoon, Aaron Mayhugh

DARAKWON

Darakwon Bldg., 211 Munbal-ro, Paju-si
Gyeonggi-do, Republic of Korea 10881
Tel : 02-736-2031 **Fax** : 02-732-2037
(Marketing Dept. ext.: 250~252, Editorial Dept. ext.: 420~426)

Copyright © 2024, by Cho Jae-hee, Kim Doe-hee, Sohn Jung-ran

All rights reserved. No part of this publication may be reproduced, stored in a retrieval
system, or transmitted in any form or by any means, electronic, mechanical, photocopying
or otherwise, without the prior consent of the copyright owner. Refund after purchase is
possible only according to the company regulations. Contact the above telephone number
for any inquiry. Consumer damages caused by loss, damage etc. can be compensated
according to consumer dispute resolution standards announced by the Korea Fair Trade
Commission. An incorrectly collated book will be exchanged.

ISBN : 978-89-277-3333-1 13710

http://www.darakwon.co.kr
http://koreanbooks.darakwon.co.kr
Visit the Darakwon homepage to learn about our other publications and
promotions and to download the contents in MP3 format.

EVERYDAY K-LINGO

Cho Jae-hee, Kim Doe-hee, Sohn Jung-ran

Learn vivid, 100% real-life Korean through fun comics!

DARAKWON

머리말

"우리 N빵하자!" "진실의 미간이 나오네!"

한국인들이 자연스럽게 자주 사용하는 이런 표현들을 얼마나 잘 알고 있나요?
유튜브의 한국어 자막이나 인스타그램의 댓글 등을 잘 이해하고 있나요?
열심히 한국어를 공부하고 있어도 뭔가 부족하다고 느끼실 겁니다.

시대에 맞는 주제 및 표현

왜냐하면 스마트 기기의 등장 이후 우리의 일상이 변화했기 때문입니다.
우리는 스마트폰의 알람 소리로 눈을 뜨고, 침대에 누운 채 SNS로 친구들과 소통을 합니다. 배달앱을 통해서 맛집의 음식을 배달해서 식사를 하고, 잠깐 짬을 내서 인터넷 쇼핑도 합니다. 단체 톡으로 친구들과 약속을 정하고 장소를 공지하고 사진도 주고받습니다. 그리고 혼자서 느긋하게 OTT를 보며 시간을 보내다가 잠이 듭니다.
이러한 변화를 반영하여 **"Everyday K-Lingo"**에서는 스마트폰, SNS, 인터넷 쇼핑, OTT, 배달앱, 카톡 등을 활용하는 "새로운 일상"을 주제로 선정하였으며 그 일상에서 빈번하게 사용되는 어휘 및 표현을 담았습니다.

낱개의 단어보다는 덩어리 표현

하지만 단어들만 많이 안다고 해서 쉽게 표현할 수 있는 건 아닙니다.
예를 들어 '최애의 인스타에 댓글을 달았어'라고 말하고 싶다면 '댓글'만 알아서는 안 됩니다. '댓글을 달다'도 알아야 하고 '인스타'와 '댓글을 달다'를 조사 '에'로 연결해야 한다는 것도 알아야 합니다. 이처럼 덩어리 단위로 기억하고 있어야 머리 속에서 떠오르는 상황이나 행동을 재빨리 한국어로 말할 수 있습니다.

이를 위해 "Everyday K-Lingo"는 낱개의 단어가 아니라 의미 덩어리로 어휘를 제시했습니다.

생생하게 살아있는 대화

새로운 어휘들은 구체적인 상황 속에서 그 사용법을 익혀야 훨씬 더 받아들이기 쉽고, 실제로 그 상황을 마주했을 때 자연스럽게 말할 수 있습니다.

이를 위해 "Everyday K-Lingo"는 다양한 상황을 싣고, 생생한 한국어 표현을 그대로 살려 대화를 구성했습니다. 또한 대화에는 '배 불러'가 아니라 '배 터질 것 같아'와 같이 보다 맛깔나는 한국어 표현과 함께 '찐맛집'과 같은 비표준어, 유행어, 신조어도 포함하고 있습니다.

특히 대화를 4컷 만화로 제시하여, 자기 전에 침대에 누워 한 편의 웹툰을 보듯이 가벼운 마음으로 읽을 수 있게 했습니다.

여러분들이 한국인을 만나서 편한 마음으로 풍성한 대화를 나눌 수 있는 데에 "Everyday K-Lingo"가 도움이 됐으면 좋겠습니다. 이 책이 디딤돌이 되어 한 단계 더 올라서서, 높게만 느껴졌던 한국어의 벽을 넘을 수 있게 되기를 바랍니다.

여러분의 한국어 학습을 응원합니다.

저자 일동

Preface

"우리 N빵하자!"
"진실의 미간이 나오네!"

How well do you know the expressions that Koreans frequently and naturally use in everyday life? Nowadays, people wake up to the sound of their smartphone alarms, stay in bed while communicating with friends through social media, have meals delivered via delivery apps, take a moment to shop online, make plans and share photos with friends in group chat rooms, and then leisurely fall asleep while watching OTT content.

Themes and Expressions Relevant to the Times

"Everyday K-Lingo" is a book designed to help learners naturally acquire vocabulary and expressions commonly used in the "new normal" of utilizing smartphones, social media, online shopping, OTT services, delivery apps, KakaoTalk, and more. It is divided into seven chapters, each focusing on various situations, further classified into four subtopics based on functional contexts. The goal is to help Korean language learners acquire Korean effortlessly, much like when they casually browse through Instagram captions or video thumbnails.

Chunks of Expressions Rather Than Individual Words

Knowing individual vocabulary and expressions doesn't necessarily mean you can easily express yourself in Korean. For instance, to say

"I commented on my favorite Instagram," knowing just the word "comment(댓글)" isn't enough. You also need to know "to comment(댓글을 달다)" and how to connect "Instagram" and "to comment" with the particle "에." By memorizing grammar elements in chunks, you can quickly speak Korean when situations or actions come to mind. **"Everyday K-Lingo"** presents vocabulary in semantic chunks to facilitate this process.

Vibrant Conversations

"Everyday K-Lingo" presents lively Korean expressions used in various situations through engaging dialogues. Especially, conversations are presented in in entertaining four-panel cartoons, allowing readers to read with a light heart, akin to reading a webtoon before bed. It also includes non-standard language, buzzword, and informal language not typically covered in books, providing readers with a rich experience of authentic Korean expressions.

We hope **"Everyday K-Lingo"** will help you comfortably engage in rich conversations with Koreans. We wish for this book to help you overcome the perceived barrier of learning Korean and cheer on your Korean language journey.

The Authors

이 책의 구성 및 활용

이 책은 총 7개 챕터와 28개의 과로 구성하였으며 각 과는 '도입 및 어휘'와 '대화'로 구성되어 있습니다. 각 챕터마다 '단원 어휘 정리'를 통해 챕터에서 학습한 어휘를 복습하고, 간단한 퀴즈를 통해 학습자가 스스로 이해도를 점검할 수 있도록 했습니다.

도입 및 어휘

의미 덩어리로 제시된 어휘들을 관련성 있는 것끼리 묶어서 제시하였습니다.

사실성 있는 그림을 함께 제시하여 어휘의 이해도를 높였습니다.

QR 코드로 음성 파일을 듣고 따라하면서 자연스러운 억양과 발음을 익힐 수 있습니다.

생생한 예문을 통해 어휘의 사용법을 더 쉽게 익힐 수 있습니다.

대화

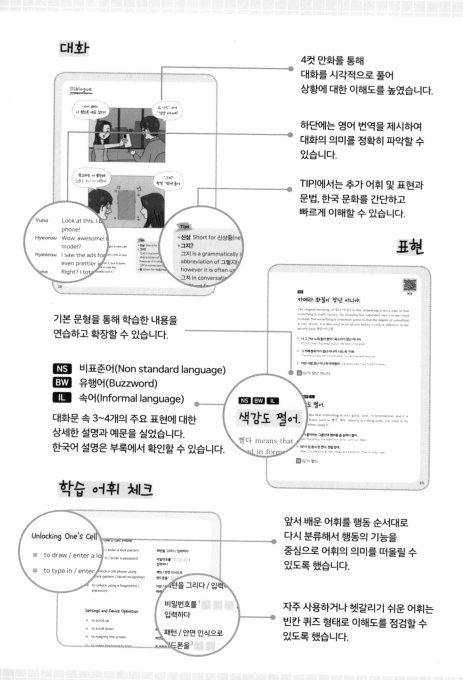

4컷 만화를 통해
대화를 시각적으로 풀어
상황에 대한 이해도를 높였습니다.

하단에는 영어 번역을 제시하여
대화의 의미를 정확히 파악할 수
있습니다.

TIP!에서는 추가 어휘 및 표현과
문법, 한국 문화를 간단하고
빠르게 이해할 수 있습니다.

표현

기본 문형을 통해 학습한 내용을
연습하고 확장할 수 있습니다.

NS 비표준어(Non standard language)
BW 유행어(Buzzword)
IL 속어(Informal language)

대화문 속 3~4개의 주요 표현에 대한
상세한 설명과 예문을 실었습니다.
한국어 설명은 부록에서 확인할 수 있습니다.

학습 어휘 체크

앞서 배운 어휘를 행동 순서대로
다시 분류해서 행동의 기능을
중심으로 어휘의 의미를 떠올릴 수
있도록 했습니다.

자주 사용하거나 헷갈리기 쉬운 어휘는
빈칸 퀴즈 형태로 이해도를 점검할 수
있도록 했습니다.

How to Use This Book

The book consists of a total of 7 chapters and 28 units, each composed of "Introduction and Vocabulary" and "Dialogue." For each chapter, a "Unit Vocabulary Review" is provided to review the vocabulary learned in the chapter, and simple quizzes are included to allow learners to check their comprehension on their own.

Introduction and Vocabulary

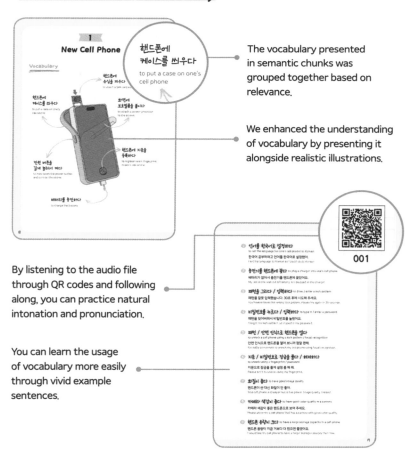

The vocabulary presented in semantic chunks was grouped together based on relevance.

We enhanced the understanding of vocabulary by presenting it alongside realistic illustrations.

By listening to the audio file through QR codes and following along, you can practice natural intonation and pronunciation.

You can learn the usage of vocabulary more easily through vivid example sentences.

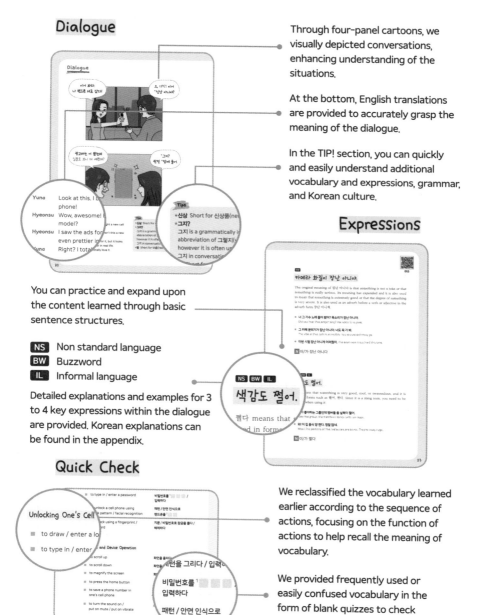

Dialogue

Through four-panel cartoons, we visually depicted conversations, enhancing understanding of the situations.

At the bottom, English translations are provided to accurately grasp the meaning of the dialogue.

In the TIP! section, you can quickly and easily understand additional vocabulary and expressions, grammar, and Korean culture.

Expressions

You can practice and expand upon the content learned through basic sentence structures.

NS Non standard language
BW Buzzword
IL Informal language

Detailed explanations and examples for 3 to 4 key expressions within the dialogue are provided. Korean explanations can be found in the appendix.

Quick Check

We reclassified the vocabulary learned earlier according to the sequence of actions, focusing on the function of actions to help recall the meaning of vocabulary.

We provided frequently used or easily confused vocabulary in the form of blank quizzes to check comprehension.

Table of Contents

Main Characters

박유나
한국인 대학원생
마엘과 함께 살며 고양이
루돌프를 키우고 있다.

이현수
한국인 직장인
알렉스와 함께 살며
퇴근 후 넷플릭스를
즐겨 본다.

루돌프
박유나의 고양이
큰 덩치와 달리 귀엽고
순한 성격이다.

료
일본인 대학원생
박유나의 대학원 동기로
친절하고 배려심이
많은 성격이다.

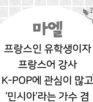

마엘
프랑스인 유학생이자
프랑스어 강사
K-POP에 관심이 많고
'민시아'라는 가수 겸
배우를 좋아한다.

잉
태국인 유학생
다정한 성격으로
스마트 기기 사용에
능숙하다.

알렉스
미국인 유학생
여유롭고 느긋한
성격으로 먹는 것을
좋아한다.

1

핸드폰을 새로 샀다!

I Bought a New Cell Phone!

New Cell Phone

Vocabulary

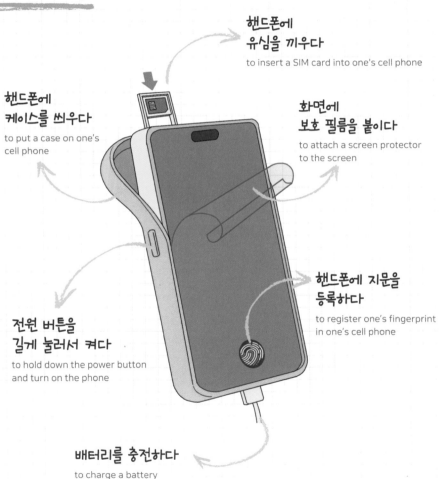

핸드폰에
유심을 끼우다
to insert a SIM card into one's cell phone

핸드폰에
케이스를 씌우다
to put a case on one's
cell phone

화면에
보호 필름을 붙이다
to attach a screen protector
to the screen

핸드폰에 지문을
등록하다
to register one's fingerprint
in one's cell phone

전원 버튼을
길게 눌러서 켜다
to hold down the power button
and turn on the phone

배터리를 충전하다
to charge a battery

① 언어를 한국어로 설정하다
to set the language (on one's cell phone) to Korean
한국어 공부하려고 언어를 한국어로 설정했어.
I set the language to Korean so I could study Korean.

② 충전기를 핸드폰에 꽂다 to plug a charger into one's cell phone
배터리가 없어서 충전기를 핸드폰에 꽂았어요.
My cell phone was out of battery, so I plugged in the charger.

③ 패턴을 그리다 / 입력하다 to draw / enter a lock pattern
패턴을 잘못 입력했습니다. 30초 후에 시도해 주세요.
You have entered the wrong lock pattern. Please try again in 30 seconds.

④ 비밀번호를 누르다 / 입력하다 to type in / enter a password
패턴을 잊어버려서 비밀번호를 눌렀어요.
I forgot my lock pattern, so I typed in my password.

⑤ 패턴 / 안면 인식으로 핸드폰을 열다
to unlock a cell phone using a lock pattern / facial recognition
안면 인식으로 핸드폰을 열어 보니까 정말 편해.
It's really convenient to unlock my cell phone using facial recognition.

⑥ 지문 / 비밀번호로 잠금을 풀다 / 해제하다
to unlock using a fingerprint / password
지문으로 잠금을 풀게 설정 좀 해 줘.
Please set it to unlock using my fingerprint.

⑦ 화질이 좋다 to have good image quality
핸드폰이 싼 대신 화질이 안 좋아.
This cell phone is cheaper but it has poorer image quality, instead.

⑧ 카메라 색감이 좋다 to have good color quality in a camera
카메라 색감이 좋은 핸드폰으로 보여 주세요.
Please show me a cell phone that has a camera with good color quality.

⑨ 핸드폰 용량이 크다 to have a large storage capacity in a cell phone
핸드폰 용량이 지금 거보다 더 컸으면 좋겠어요.
I would like my cell phone to have a larger storage capacity than now.

Dialogue

Yuna	Look at this. I bought a new cell phone!
Hyeonsu	Wow, awesome! Isn't this a new model?
Hyeonsu	I saw the ads for it, but it looks even prettier in real life.
Yuna	Right? I totally love it.

Tips

★신상 Short for 신상품(new product)

★그지?
그지 is a grammatically incorrect abbreviation of 그렇지(yes, isn't it?), however it is often used as 그지, 그치 in conversation.

★맘 Short for 마음(heart, feelings)

Tips

*근데
Short for 그런데(but, however)

Hyeonsu	But why haven't you put a case on it or attached a screen protector yet?
Yuna	I haven't been able to choose one that I like yet. I'm still deciding.
Hyeonsu	Unlock your phone. Let's see what's in it.
Yuna	There's not much in it. But the camera quality is no joke.
Hyeonsu	Ooh, it has dope color quality, too.

NS **BW**

대박!

The original meaning of 대박 is a large success, so if one says 대박이 나다, it means "to achieve a great success." Recently, the meaning of 대박 has expanded to be used as an exclamation to indicate that something is mind-blowing, or that something is good or amazing. 대박 can be used in the form N이/가 대박이다. It can also be used as an adverb meaning "very (much)."

- A: 이거 내가 만든 케이크야. 예쁘지? I made this cake. Isn't it pretty?
  B: 대박! 이걸 직접 만들었다고? Amazing! You made this yourself?

- 나 이 핸드폰 대박 싸게 샀다. I bought this cell phone for super cheap.

- 이번에 새로 나온 영화 완전 대박이야. The newly released movie is totally awesome.

실물로 보니 더 예쁜데?

실물로 보다 means to see person or object that was seen in a picture or on a screen in real life, and 실물로 보니(까) is often followed by how one felt, or something one newly learned, when seeing the person/object in reality.

- 실물로 보니 앱에서 본 것보다 방이 좀 작네요.
  Now that I've seen it in person, the room is a bit smaller than it looked on the app.

- 그 배우 실물로 보니까 훨씬 더 멋있었어.
  I've seen that actor in person, and he was way cooler than he looked on the screen.

- 화면에서 봤을 때는 예뻐 보였는데 실물로 보니 별로네.
  It looked pretty when I saw it on the screen, but it doesn't look that good in real life.

실물로 보니(까)

카메라 화질이 장난 아니야.

The original meaning of 장난 아니다 is that something is not a joke or that something is really serious. Its meaning has expanded and it is also used to mean that something is extremely good or that the degree of something is very severe. It is also used as an adverb before a verb or adjective in the adverb form 장난 아니게.

● **너 그 가수 노래 들어 봤어? 목소리가 장난 아니야.**
Did you hear that singer sing? Her voice is no joke.

● **그 카페 분위기가 장난 아니야. 너도 꼭 가 봐.**
The vibe at that café is incredible. You should definitely go.

● **이번 시험 장난 아니게 어려웠어.** The exam was crazy hard this time.

N 이/가 장난 아니다

색감도 쩔어.

쩔다 means that something is very good, cool, or tremendous, and it is used in forms such as 쩔어, 쩐다. Since it is a slang term, you need to be careful when using it.

● **내가 좋아하는 그룹인데 멤버들 춤 실력이 쩔어.**
I like this group; the members' dance skills are dope.

● **와! 이 집 음식 양 쩐다. 정말 많네.**
Wow! The portions at this restaurant are bomb. They're really huge.

N 이/가 쩔다

Using a Cell Phone

Vocabulary

와이파이 Wi-fi

{ 와이파이가 연결이 (안) 되다
for the wi-fi to (not) be connected

{ 와이파이가 안 뜨다
for the wi-fi to not show up

4:30
5월 4일 토요일

와이파이   소리   블루투스   새로

비행기 모드 카드 모드 절전 모드   모바일
데이터

블루투스 Bluetooth

{ 블루투스로 이어폰을 연결하다
to connect earphones via Bluetooth

{ 블루투스 연결이 자주 끊기다
for the Bluetooth to be disconnected
often

홈 버튼을 누르다
to press the home button

데이터 Cellular Data

{ 데이터를 켜다
to turn on cellular data

{ 데이터를 끄다
to turn off cellular data

{ 데이터를 사용하다
to use cellular data

① **핸드폰을 하다** to use one's cell phone

수업 시간에는 핸드폰을 하지 마세요.
Don't use your cell phone during class time.

② **화면을 올리다** to scroll up

A: 식당 연락처가 어디 있지? Where's the phone number for the restaurant?
B: 아, 나 본 것 같은데⋯⋯. 화면 좀 다시 올려 봐. Ah, I think I saw it⋯. Scroll up again.

③ **화면을 내리다** to scroll down

화면을 좀 더 내리면 식당 홈페이지 링크가 나올 거야.
If you scroll down a bit more, the link to the restaurant's website will come up.

④ **화면을 확대하다** to magnify the screen

글씨가 너무 작은데 화면 좀 확대해 봐.
The font is so small. Zoom in a bit.

⑤ **전화번호를 핸드폰에 저장하다** to save a phone number in one's cell phone

여행 가기 전에 호텔 전화번호를 미리 핸드폰에 저장했다.
Before I left on my trip, I saved the hotel's phone number in my cell phone.

⑥ **소리 / 무음 / 진동으로 바꾸다**
to turn the sound on / put on mute / put on vibrate

도서관에 있어서 핸드폰을 무음으로 바꿨어요.
I'm in the library, so I put my cell phone on mute.

⑦ **데이터로 영상을 보다** to watch a video using cellular data

데이터로 영상을 많이 봤더니 데이터가 많이 안 남았어.
I watched a lot of videos using my cellular data, so I don't have a lot of data left.

⑧ **와이파이 비밀번호를 입력하다** to enter the wi-fi password

나 여기 와이파이 비밀번호를 입력한 적이 있나 봐. 바로 연결되네.
I must have entered the wi-fi password here before. It connected right away.

Dialogue

Alex	Oh my gosh! I was using cellular data until now.
Yuna	Connect to the wi-fi right away.
Alex	What's the password for the wi-fi here?
Yuna	It's written there on the receipt.

Tips

★**얼른** quickly, right away
★**쓰여 있다** to be written

Alex   Huh? Weird. Why won't the wi-fi connect?

Yuna   Could it be that you entered the password incorrectly? Try again.

Alex   Ah! That was a 9, not a "g." Now it's connected.

NS BW

헐!

헐 is an exclamation used in surprising or ridiculous situations.

● 헐! 커피 한 잔에 7,000원이나 해. Whoa! One cup of coffee is 7,000 won.

● 이걸 오늘까지 다 해야 한다고? 헐! I have to do all of this by today? Oh my gosh!

● A: 잉이랑 료랑 사귄대. I heard that Ing and Ryo are dating.
  B: 헐! 진짜? Whoa! Really?

잘못 입력한 거 아니야?

잘못 입력한 거 아니야? in this dialogue isn't really a question, but rather means that it seems the subject entered the password incorrectly. As such, using A/V은/는 거 아니야? is a way to gently express one's thoughts by turning them into the negative form of a question.

● 그 사람이 너 좋아하는 거 아니야? Doesn't that person like you?

● 이거 너무 비싼 거 아니야? 더 싼 게 있을 것 같은데.
  Isn't this too expensive? I think there's a cheaper one.

● 오는 길에 무슨 일 생긴 거 아니야?
  Something happened on the way, didn't it?

A/V 은/는 거 아니야?

g가 아니라 9네.

A는 B가 아니에요. A는 C예요(A is not B. A is C.) is shortened to (A는) B가 아니라 C예요((A is) not B; it's C). A is often omitted from the expression.

- *걔는 여자 친구가 아니라 내 동생이야.
  She's not my girlfriend; she's my little sister.

- 약속 장소는 2번 출구가 아니라 3번 출구야.
  The meeting place isn't exit 2; it's exit 3.

- 약속은 오늘이 아니라 내일이야.
  The appointment isn't today; it's tomorrow.

 은/는 이/가 아니라 이다

> **Tips**
>
> *걔
> 걔 is short for 그 아이.
> It is usually used when referring to a friend or someone who is younger. 얘 is short for 이 아이, and 쟤 is short for 저 아이.

3

Using an App

Vocabulary

앱을 핸드폰에 깔다 / 설치하다 / 다운받다
to download / install an app on one's cell phone

앱을 업데이트하다
to update an app

앱을 핸드폰에서 지우다 / 제거하다 / 삭제하다
to erase / delete an app from one's cell phone

앱으로 일정을 관리하다
to manage one's schedule using an app

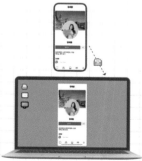

앱이 노트북과 연동이 되다
for an app to be linked with one's laptop

앱을 홈 화면에 추가하다
to add an app to the home screen

007

① 앱을 열다 / 켜다 to open an app

앱을 열 때마다 로그인을 새로 해야 해. 이상하네.
Every time I open the app, I have to log in again. How strange.

② 앱에 들어가다 to go into an app

지도 앱에 들어가서 교통편을 검색해 봐.
Go into the map app and search for the means of transportation.

③ 앱을 닫다 / 끄다 to close an app

사용한 후에는 앱을 바로 닫는 게 좋아. It's good to close an app right after you use it.

④ 앱을 쓰다 / 사용하다 to use an app

이 앱을 써 보니까 편하더라. Now that I've tried using this app, things are more convenient.

⑤ 앱이 안 열리다 for an app to not open

아까부터 앱이 안 열려서 확인을 못 하고 있어.
Since earlier, the app won't open, so I'm not able to check it.

⑥ 앱에 안 들어가지다 to be unable to go into an app

돈을 보내야 하는데 은행 앱에 안 들어가져.
I have to send some money, but I can't go into the bank app.

⑦ 앱이 작동이 안 되다 for an app to not work

앱이 한 번 멈춘 후부터 계속 작동이 안 돼요.
The app stopped working once, and since then it still won't work.

⑧ 앱이 튕기다 for an app to suddenly close

앱이 갑자기 튕겨서 쓰고 있던 메일이 다 지워졌어.
The app suddenly closed, so the email I was writing was all deleted.

⑨ 앱이 버벅거리다 for an app to glitch

A: 왜 이렇게 앱이 버벅거리지? Why is the app glitching like this?
B: 그럼 지웠다가 다시 깔아 봐. Then try deleting it and downloading it again.

Dialogue

요즘 해야 할 일들을 *자꾸 *깜빡깜빡해.

왜? 할 일이 많아?

많다기보다는 일정이 그날그날 달라서 헷갈려.

Tips

*자꾸 repeatedly
*깜빡깜빡하다
    to flicker, to repeatedly forget

Alex These days, I keep forgetting the things I have to do.

Ing Why? Do you have a lot to do?

Alex It's not that I have a lot to do; I just get confused because my schedule is different every day.

008

Ing	Don't you use a scheduling app?
Alex	I used one before, but after I updated it, the app kept closing, so I deleted it.
Ing	The one I use is pretty good. You should try using it.
Alex	Oh! I like this app way better, because it gives me a neat, at-a-glance view of my schedule.
Ing	Right? You should download and use this app, too.

33

(일정이) 많다기보다는 헷갈려.

많다기보다는 헷갈려 means that rather than having a lot on one's schedule, the person is getting confused about their schedule. Although A/V다기보다는 includes the particle 보다 which indicates comparison, this expression does not compare the preceding and following content; rather, it is an expression that negates the preceding content and indicates that the following content is more appropriate.

- **그 수업은 재미있다기보다는 도움이 되는 수업이야.**
  That class is more helpful than fun.

- **운동을 잘한다기보다는 운동하는 걸 좋아해.** I like exercise more than I am good at it.

- **화가 났다기보다는 피곤해서 그래요.** It's because I was tired, not because I was angry.

A/V 다기보다는 ▨▨▨▨▨▨

그날그날 달라서 헷갈려.

그날그날 다르다 means that something varies from day to day, without being fixed.

- **콘서트 시간이 그날그날 다르대.**
  They say that the concert time is different from day to day.

- **이 식당은 메뉴가 그날그날 달라져.**
  The menu at this restaurant changes from day to day.

- **일정이 그날그날 달라서 언제 시간이 날지 잘 모르겠어요.**
  My schedule is different from day to day, so I'm not sure when I will have time.

N 이/가 그날그날 다르다

009

한눈에 보여서 훨씬 좋네.

한눈 refers to a range that the eye can see all at once, so 한눈에 보이다 means that one can easily grasp something even after seeing it only one time. This expression is also used in the forms 한눈에 볼 수 있다 and 한눈에 들어오다.

- **오늘 수업 내용을 한눈에 보이게 정리했어.**
  I summed up the content from today's class so I can see it all at a glance.

- **여기 서서 보니 서울 시내가 한눈에 들어오네.**
  Standing here, I can see all of downtown Seoul at once.

- **서울에 있는 맛집을 한눈에 볼 수 있는 앱이 없을까?**
  Isn't there an app where one can see all the famous restaurants in Seoul at once?

N 이/가 한눈에 보이다

Cell Phone Problems

Vocabulary

핸드폰에 보조 배터리를 연결하다
to connect one's cell phone to an external battery

핸드폰 저장 공간이 부족하다
to lack storage space on one's cell phone

액정이 깨지다
for the screen to be broken

핸드폰이 뜨거워지다
for the cell phone to become hot

핸드폰을 떨어뜨리다
to drop one's cell phone

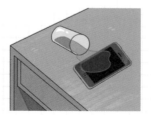

핸드폰에 물을 쏟다
to spill water on one's cell phone

① 배터리가 빨리 닳다 for the battery to run out quickly

- 요즘 배터리가 빨리 닳아서 보조 배터리를 가지고 다녀.
These days, the battery runs out so quickly that I carry an external battery around with me.

② 배터리가 나가다 / 다 떨어지다 / 다 닳다 to run out of battery

갑자기 배터리가 다 떨어져서 사진도 많이 못 찍었어.
I suddenly ran out of battery, so I couldn't take a lot of pictures.

③ 배터리가 30% 남다 to have 30% battery left

배터리가 30%밖에 안 남았네. 어서 충전해야겠다.
I only have 30% battery left. I should charge it quickly.

④ 전원이 안 켜지다 for the power to not turn on

전원 버튼을 길게 눌러도 전원이 안 켜져요.
Even when I hold down the power button, it doesn't turn on.

⑤ 핸드폰이 자꾸 꺼지다 for one's cell phone to keep turning off

핸드폰을 떨어뜨린 후부터 이유 없이 핸드폰이 자꾸 꺼져.
Ever since I dropped my cell phone, it keeps turning off for no reason.

⑥ 핸드폰이 느려지다 for one's cell phone to become slow

새 걸로 바꿔야 할 것 같아. 핸드폰이 너무 느려졌어.
I think I need to get a new phone. My phone has gotten way too slow.

⑦ 화면이 갑자기 멈추다 for the screen to suddenly freeze

화면이 갑자기 멈춰서 핸드폰을 껐다가 다시 켰어요.
The screen suddenly froze, so I turned my phone off and turned it back on again.

⑧ 화면이 안 넘어가다 for the screen to not move

버튼을 눌렀는데도 화면이 안 넘어가요.
I pressed the button, but the screen won't move.

Dialogue

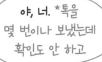

Mael	Hey, you. I sent you KakaoTalk messages multiple times, but you haven't even looked at them.
Ryo	Really? Huh? My cell phone is off. The battery must have run out. Sorry. I didn't know.
Mael	That's why you should charge your phone in advance before you go out.
Ryo	When I left this morning, I definitely had 80% left. But these days, the battery seems to run out strangely fast.

Tips

★톡을 보내다

톡 is short for KakaoTalk, the most commonly used messenger app in Korea. 톡을 보내다 means that one sent a message via KakaoTalk.

Tips

★한 about, approximately

Ryo	Maybe it's because my phone is old.
Mael	How long ago did you buy it?
Ryo	I'm not sure. I think it's been more than 3 years or so.
Mael	Then it's time for you to get rid of it. Get a new phone.
Ryo	Ah, why? It's still good enough to use.

톡을 몇 번이나 보냈는데 확인도 안 하고.

몇 번이나 V았/었는데 is used when emphasizing that one has frequently done a certain action multiple times. In the clause after V았/었는데, the results that come are different from what was expected from that action. As such, this expression contains feelings of disappointment, annoyance, or anger.

- **전화를 몇 번이나 했는데 왜 안 받아?**
  I called you several times; why didn't you pick up?

- **내가 몇 번이나 말했는데 또 잊어버렸어?**
  I told you multiple times, but you forgot again?

- **몇 번이나 확인했는데 실수가 나왔어.**
  I checked multiple times, but there were still mistakes.

몇 번이나 **V** 았/었는데

오래돼서 그런가?

A/V아/어서 그런가? is used when guessing whether a certain result may have been due to a certain reason. It takes the form of a question but doesn't require an answer from the other person.

- **잘 못 자서 그런가? 요즘 좀 피곤하네.**
  I wonder if it's because I'm not sleeping well. I'm a bit tired these days.

- **이 메뉴는 별로 인기가 없네. 너무 비싸서 그런가?**
  This dish isn't very popular. Could it be because it's too expensive?

● **A: 길이 대박 막히네.** Traffic is freaking awful.

B: 그렇네. 주말에 놀러가는 사람이 많아서 그런가?
Seriously. I wonder if it's because a lot of people are heading out for the weekend.

A/V 아/어서 그런가?

BW

보내 줄 때도 됐네.

보내 주다 usually means that one allows someone to leave freely, and if one says 보내 줄 때도 됐다 about a certain object, it means that the object is so old that one should stop using it or throw it away.

● **노트북 산 지 10년이나 됐으니까 이제 보내 줄 때도 됐네.** It's been about 10 years since I bought this laptop, so it's about time to get rid of it now.

● **선물로 받아서 그동안 못 버리고 있었는데 이제 보내 줄 때도 된 것 같아요.**
I received this as a gift, so I haven't been able to throw it away all this time, but I think I can let it go now.

● **7년 동안 옷장에만 있던 자켓. 이제는 보내 줄 때도 된 것 같다.** This jacket has been sitting in my closet for 7 years. I think I should get rid of it now.

N 을/를 보내 줄 때도 됐다

Quick Check

Using a Cell Phone

■ to use one's cell phone   핸드폰을 [1] 하 다

Cell Phone Specifications

■ to have good image quality   화질이 좋다

■ to have good color quality in a camera   카메라 색감이 좋다

■ to have a large storage capacity in a cell phone   핸드폰 용량이 크다

Setting up After Purchasing

■ to insert a SIM card into one's cell phone   핸드폰에 유심을 [2] ▨ ▨ ▨

■ to attach a screen protector to the screen   화면에 보호 필름을 붙이다

■ to put a case on one's cell phone   핸드폰에 케이스를 씌우다

■ to hold down the power button and turn on the phone   전원 버튼을 길게 눌러서 켜다

■ to set the language (on one's cell phone) to Korean   언어를 한국어로 [3] ▨ ▨ ▨ ▨

■ to register one's fingerprint in one's cell phone   핸드폰에 [4] ▨ ▨ 을 등록하다

1 하다   2 끼우다   3 설정하다   4 지문

42

Unlocking One's Cell Phone

- to draw / enter a lock pattern

  패턴을 그리다 / 입력하다

- to type in / enter a password

  비밀번호를 [1] ⬜⬜⬜ /
  입력하다

- to unlock a cell phone using
  a lock pattern / facial recognition

  패턴 / 안면 인식으로
  핸드폰을 [2] ⬜⬜

- to unlock using a fingerprint /
  password

  지문 / 비밀번호로 잠금을 풀다 /
  해제하다

Settings and Device Operation

- to scroll up

  화면을 올리다

- to scroll down

  화면을 내리다

- to magnify the screen

  화면을 [3] ⬜⬜⬜⬜

- to press the home button

  홈 버튼을 누르다

- to save a phone number in
  one's cell phone

  전화번호를 핸드폰에
  [4] ⬜⬜⬜⬜

- to turn the sound on /
  put on mute / put on vibrate

  소리 / 무음 / [5] ⬜⬜ 으로 바꾸다

- to set one's cell phone to
  airplane mode

  핸드폰을 비행기 모드로 설정하다

1 누르다 2 열다 3 확대하다 4 저장하다 5 진동

Connecting to Wi-fi and Bluetooth

■ for the wi-fi to not show up
와이파이가 [1]

■ for the wi-fi to (not) be connected
와이파이가 연결이 (안) 되다

■ to enter the wi-fi password
와이파이 비밀번호를
[2]

■ to connect earphones
via Bluetooth
블루투스로 이어폰을
[3]

■ for the Bluetooth to be disconnected
often
블루투스 연결이 자꾸 [4]

Cellular Data

■ to turn on cellular data
데이터를 켜다

■ to turn off cellular data
데이터를 끄다

■ to use cellular data
데이터를 사용하다

■ to watch a video using
cellular data
데이터로 영상을 보다

Applications/Apps

■ to download / install an app on
one's cell phone
앱을 핸드폰에 [5] /
설치하다 / 다운받다

■ to open an app
앱을 열다 / 켜다

1 안 뜨다 2 입력하다 3 연결하다 4 끊기다 5 깔다

▪ to go into an app	앱에 들어가다	
▪ to close an app	앱을 [1] / 끄다	
▪ to use an app	앱을 쓰다 / 사용하다	
▪ to update an app	앱을 업데이트하다	
▪ to erase / delete an app from one's cell phone	앱을 핸드폰에서 [2] / 제거하다 / 삭제하다	
▪ to manage one's schedule using an app	앱으로 일정을 관리하다	
▪ for an app to not open	앱이 안 열리다	
▪ to be unable to go into an app	앱에 안 들어가지다	
▪ for an app to not work	앱이 작동이 안 되다	
▪ for an app to suddenly close	앱이 튕기다	
▪ for an app to glitch	앱이 버벅거리다	
▪ for an app to be linked with one's laptop	앱이 노트북과 [3] 이 되다	
▪ to add an app to the home screen	앱을 홈 화면에 추가하다	

Battery

▪ to charge a battery	배터리를 [4]	
▪ to plug a charger into one's cell phone	충전기를 핸드폰에 [5]	

1 닫다 2 지우다 3 연동 4 충전하다 5 꽂다

45

■	for the battery to run out quickly	배터리가 빨리 닳다
■	to run out of battery	배터리가 [1] ▨▨▨ / 다 떨어지다 / 다 닳다
■	to have 30% battery left	배터리가 30% 남다
■	to connect one's cell phone to an external battery	핸드폰에 보조 배터리를 연결하다

Problems that Arise While Using a Cell Phone

■	for the power to not turn on	전원이 안 켜지다
■	for one's cell phone to keep turning off	핸드폰이 자꾸 [2] ▨▨▨
■	for one's cell phone to become slow	핸드폰이 느려지다
■	for the screen to be broken	[3] ▨▨ 이 깨지다
■	for the screen to suddenly freeze	화면이 갑자기 멈추다
■	for the screen to not move	화면이 안 넘어가다
■	to lack storage space on one's cell phone	핸드폰 저장 공간이 부족하다
■	for the cell phone to become hot	핸드폰이 뜨거워지다
■	to drop one's cell phone	핸드폰을 [4] ▨▨▨▨▨
■	to spill water on one's cell phone	핸드폰에 물을 쏟다

1 나가다 2 꺼지다 3 액정 4 떨어뜨리다

2

나도 SNS 한번 해 볼까?

Should I Try Using Social Media Too?

Starting to Use Instagram

Vocabulary

계정 Account

{ 계정을 만들다 / 파다 / 개설하다
to make / open / establish an account

{ 계정을 공개로 하다
to make an account public

친구를 팔로우하다
to follow a friend

팔로워 수가 많다
to have a lot of followers

*프사를 바꾸다
to change one's profile picture

프로필에 링크를 걸다
to set up a link to one's profile

친구에게 DM을 보내다
to send a DM to a friend

Tips

*프사
Short for 프로필 사진(profile picture)

48

013

① 계정을 운영하다 to run an account

저희 카페에서 운영하고 있는 인스타 계정에서 오늘의 메뉴를 확인해 주세요.
Please check today's menu on the Instagram account being run by our café.

② 계정을 비공개로 하다 / 돌리다 to make / turn an account private

어떤 사람이 자꾸 이상한 댓글을 달아서 계정을 비공개로 돌렸어.
Someone keeps leaving strange comments, so I made my account private.

③ 팔로우를 취소하다 to stop following (someone's account)

친구가 갑자기 팔로우를 취소했는데 이유를 모르겠어.
My friend suddenly stopped following me, but I don't know why.

④ 계정을 지우다 / 삭제하다 to remove / delete one's account

남자 친구와 헤어진 후 계정을 지우고 새 계정을 만들었어.
After breaking up with my boyfriend, I deleted my account and made a new one.

⑤ 계정을 탈퇴하다 to close one's account

나 SNS 끊었어. 인스타 계정도 탈퇴했어.
I quit using social media. I closed my Instagram account, too.

⑥ 계정을 차단하다 to block an account

DM으로 이상한 광고를 자꾸 보내서 계정을 차단했어.
That person kept sending me DMs with weird ads, so I blocked their account.

⑦ 계정이 친구한테 차단당하다 to have one's account blocked by a friend

A: 요즘 친구 피드가 안 보여. 왜 그러지?
  I don't see my friend's feed these days. I wonder why?
B: 그 친구한테 계정 차단당한 거 아니야?
  Could that mean you were blocked by that friend?

Dialogue

내 *최애 드디어 이번에 *인스타 계정 만들었어!

민시아
1590만 팔로워

그래? 사진은 자주 올라와?

응. 일주일에 세 번은 올라오고 지난주에는 *라방도 했어.

민시아

Mael   My bias finally made an Instagram account!

Hyeonsu   Really? Does she upload pictures often?

Mael   Yeah. She uploads 3 times a week, and last week she even did a live broadcast.

Tips

★최애
This means the person or things that one loves the most, and it is often used to indicate one's favorite member of an idol group.

★인스타 Short for 인스타그램 (Instagram)

★라방 Short for 라이브 방송 (live broadcast)

Hyeonsu	You should leave a comment. Who knows? She might leave you a reply.
Mael	There are so many comments on her feed; you think she'd actually read my comment?
Mael	That's why I sent her a DM.
Hyeonsu	Hey, that's enough. You're going to get yourself blocked.

답글 남겨 줄지 누가 알아?

누가 알아? is an expression that means no one knows whether a certain event might happen, and is used when saying that although the possibility is small, it is not impossible. It is connected with A/V을지 before it.

- 좋아하면 한번 연락해 봐. 그 사람도 너한테 관심 있을지 누가 알아? If you like her, try contacting her. Who knows? Maybe that person is interested in you, too.

- 우리 복권이나 사 볼까? 당첨될지 누가 알아?
  Should we buy a lottery ticket? Who knows if we might win?

- 가격이나 물어보자. 생각보다 쌀지 누가 알아?
  Let's ask for the price. It might be cheaper than we think.

A/V 을지 누가 알아?

댓글이 얼마나 많은데 내 거 읽기나 하겠어?

댓글이 얼마나 많은데 is an expression emphasizing that there are a lot of comments, and 읽기나 하겠어? expresses in the form of a question that there is absolutely no possibility the comments will be read. Therefore, N 이/가 얼마나 많은데 V기나 하겠어? can be used when there is too much of something, so there is almost no possibility of it happening.

- 할 일이 얼마나 많은데 영화 볼 시간이 있기나 하겠어? I have so much work to do; You think I have time to watch a movie?

- 그 수업 듣는 학생들이 얼마나 많은데 교수님이 내 이름을 알기나 하겠어?
  There are so many students attending that class. There's no way the professor would know my name.

N 이/가 얼마나 많은데 **V** 기나 하겠어?

015

적당히 해라.

적당히 means appropriately or moderately, indicating doing something to an appropriate extent without going overboard. 적당히 해라 is an expression advising to stop because something is excessive. It serves as advice or warning to stay appropriate boundaries and act with moderation.

- 너 때문에 분위기 안 좋아졌잖아. 적당히 해.
  The atmosphere grew worse because of you. That's enough.

- A: 피곤해서 죽겠어. I'm dead tired.
  B: 또 밤새 게임한 거야? 적당히 해라.
  Did you stay up all night playing games again? Give it a rest.

N 을/를 적당히 해(라).

그러다가 차단당한다.

그러다가 차단당한다 is a warning that continuing the action in the preceding sentence may lead to negative results, such as being blocked. 그러다가(는) means that if one continues the previous action, bad results may occur, and this expression is used to advise against it or warn of potential consequences.

- 또 누워서 핸드폰 봐? 너 그러다가 눈 나빠져. You're lying down and looking at your cell phone again? If you keep doing that, your eyesight is going to get worse.

- 커피 좀 그만 마셔. 그러다가 밤에 잠 못 잔다.
  Stop drinking coffee. At this rate, you won't be able to sleep at night.

- 운전하면서 핸드폰 보지 마. 그러다가 사고 난다. Don't look at your phone while you're driving. If you do that, you're going to get in an accident.

그러다가(는) **negative outcome**

2

Instagram Posts

Vocabulary

인스타에 사진 / 글 / 피드 / 게시물을 올리다
to upload a picture / text / feed / post to Instagram

좋아요 Like

{ 게시물에 좋아요를 누르다
to press "like" on a post

{ 게시물에 좋아요 수가 많다
to have a lot of "likes" on a post

게시물을 저장하다
to save a post

고양이라고 해시태그를 달다
to use a cat hashtag

게시물에 댓글을 달다
to leave a comment on a post

댓글에 답글을 남기다
to leave a reply to a comment

016

① 인스타에 들어가다 to go into Instagram

시간이 나면 습관적으로 인스타에 들어가게 돼.
When I have time, I habitually end up going into Instagram.

② 인스타를 하다 to use Instagram

A: 너 인스타해? Do you use Instagram?
B: 계정은 있는데 거의 안 해. I have an account, but I hardly use it.

③ 인스타에서 라이브 방송을 하다 to hold a live broadcast on Instagram

좋아하는 작가가 오늘 밤 인스타에서 라이브 방송을 한대.
I heard that the author I like is holding a live broadcast on Instagram tonight.

④ 게시물에 친구를 태그하다 to tag a friend in a post

이 사진에 너 태그해도 돼?
May I tag you in this picture?

⑤ 알림을 켜다 / 알림 설정을 하다
to turn on notifications / set up the notification setting

좋아하는 가수의 라방을 놓치지 않으려고 알림 설정을 해 뒀어.
I set up a notification so I don't miss it when the singer I like holds a live broadcast.

⑥ 알림을 끄다 / 알림 설정을 해제하다
to turn off notifications / the notification setting

댓글이 너무 많이 달려서 알림을 껐어.
There are so many comments being left, so I turned off my notifications.

⑦ 피드에 악플이 많이 달리다 to have a lot of malicious comments on one's feed

지난번에 올린 피드에 이상하게 악플이 많이 달렸어.
Strangely, the feed I uploaded last time has a lot of malicious comments on it.

⑧ 악플을 신고하다 to report a malicious comment

내용이 너무 심해서 악플을 신고했다.
The content is too extreme, so I reported the malicious comment.

Dialogue

super_yuna

좋아요 10,621개

Super_yuna 우리 루돌프. 무슨 생각하니?

멍 때려도 귀여워. **통통해도 귀여워.**

*집사가 많이 사랑해.

#고양이 #멍 #애교쟁이 #내사랑루돌프

super_yuna My dear Rudolph. What are you thinking about? You're so cute even when you space out. You are adorable even though you're chubby. I love you so much.

#cat #spacedout #cutiepie #myloverudolph

Tips

★**집사**
집사 usually means butler, but people who raise cats use it to mean the owner of a cat.

56

super_yuna

댓글 53개 모두 보기

fairday
답글 달기
표정 심각한 거 보니 저녁 메뉴 생각하나 봐요.

amj_chae
답글 달기
우리 루돌프 어쩜 이래?
안 예쁜 데가 하나도 없네.

sweet.jh
답글 달기
심쿵. 루돌프 넘 귀여워요.

fairday	Judging by his serious expression, he must be thinking about dinner menu.
amj_chae	Look at you, Rudolph! There's not a single thing about you that isn't pretty.
sweet.jh	My heart! Rudolph is so cute.

NS **IL**

멍 때려도 귀여워.

멍하다 means that one is in a state without any thoughts. 멍 때리다 means one is spacing out and because it is a crude expression, one must be careful while using this expression. In this regard, a new word 불멍 was coined from 불을 보면서 멍 때리다 and 물멍 from 물을 보면서 멍 때리다. It means that one is relaxing and unwinding without any thoughts while comfortably gazing at fire or water for healing purposes.

- 졸려서 수업 시간 내내 멍 때렸어.
  I was sleepy, so I zoned out throughout the whole class time.

- 버스에서 멍 때리다가 정류장을 지나쳤어. I spaced out on the bus and missed my stop.

- 이번 주말에는 캠핑 가서 불멍하고 싶다!
  This weekend, I want to go camping and zone out in front of the campfire!

멍(을) 때리다

어쩜 이래?

어쩜 is short for 어쩌면. 어쩜 이래 is an exclamation that is used when one looks at something and wishes to express how unbelievably great, cool, or cute it is.

- 여기 어쩜 이래? 여기 있는 거 다 사고 싶다.
  Can you believe this place? I want to buy everything here.

- 이 집 케이크 어쩜 이래? 정말 달고 맛있다.
  Can you believe the cakes here? They're really sweet and delicious.

- 오늘 날씨가 어쩜 이러냐? 너무 좋다. Can you believe this weather? It's so great.

안 예쁜 데가 하나도 없네.

When the negative 안 and 하나도 없다 are used together, it conveys a strong sense of affirmation. As such, 안 예쁜 데가 하나도 없네 means that every part or place is pretty.

- 오랜만에 운동했더니 안 아픈 데가 하나도 없네.
  I worked out for the first time in a while, so there isn't a single place where I'm not sore.

- 너 안 가 본 데가 하나도 없구나. 여행 정말 많이 다녔네.
  There's no place that you haven't been, huh? You've really traveled a lot.

- 서울은 집값이 안 비싼 데가 하나도 없네.
  There is not a single place in Seoul where housing isn't expensive.

안 A/V 은/는 데가 하나도 없다

NS

심쿵

심장이 쿵 내려앉다, 쿵쿵 뛰다 are expressions that are used when one is surprised in a negative situation. 심쿵 originated from these phrases, but unlike its original meaning, it is used when one sees something so cute or cool that it makes one's heart is stolen or that one's heart skips a beat. It can be used in the forms 심쿵 or 심쿵하다 .

- 저 배우 너무 멋있지? 미소가 완전 심쿵이야.
  That actor is so cool, right? His smile is totally heart-stopping.

- 자는 모습이 너무 귀여운 우리 강아지. 볼 때마다 심쿵합니다. My puppy looks so cute when she sleeps. Every time I look at her, my heart skips a beat.

- 어제 그 드라마 봤어? 두 사람이 키스하는 장면에서 나 완전 심쿵했어. Did you see that drama yesterday? My heart totally fluttered at the couple's kissing scene.

3

Using Instagram

Vocabulary

**인스타에 사진이
새로 올라오다**

new pictures are uploaded
to Instagram

해시태그를 검색하다

to search a hashtag

릴스를 찍다

to film a reel

**인스타에 광고가
많이 뜨다**

many ads appear on
Instagram

**인스타로 새 제품을
홍보하다**

to promote a new product on
Instagram

인스타로 공구하다

to make a group
purchase using Instagram

① **피드가 삭제되다** one's feed is deleted

다시 보려고 들어갔는데 피드가 삭제됐더라.
I went to look at it again, but the feed was deleted.

② **댄스 챌린지가 유행이다** a dance challenge is trending

A: 요즘 댄스 챌린지가 유행이래.
I heard that dance challenges are trending these days.
B: 우리도 한번 해 볼까?
Should we try it, too?

③ **인스타 감성이다** to be Instagrammable

A: 와, 이 카페 분위기 완전 인스타 감성이다!
Wow, the vibe of this café is totally Instagrammable!
B: 그러게. 진짜 멋있다. 근데 가격이 너무 비싼데.
Seriously. It's so cool. But the price is too expensive.

④ **인스타 각이다** to be Instagram-worthy

A: 이 케이크 너무 예쁘다. 완전 인스타 각인데.
This cake is so pretty. It's totally Instagram-worthy.
B: 사진 찍게 먹지 말고 잠깐 기다려 봐.
Wait a second and don't eat it yet so I can take a picture.

Dialogue

내가 어제 루돌프 짱 귀여운 사진 인스타에 올린 거 봤어?

내가 좋아요도 눌렀는데 못 봤어?

알림 설정을 해제해 놔서 몰랐어.

요즘 루돌프 사진에 좋아요 수가 폭발이거든

루돌프가 반전 매력이 있지. *덩치는 큰데 *애교가 넘치잖아.

Yuna	Did you see the super cute picture of Rudolph that I uploaded to Instagram yesterday?
Ing	I even liked the picture. You didn't see it?
Yuna	I didn't know because I turned off my notifications.
Yuna	These days, the number of likes on Rudolph's pictures has exploded.
Ing	Rudolph has unexpected charm. He's big, but he's such a cutie.

Tips

★덩치가 크다 to have a large build
★애교가 넘치다 to be full of charm

020

Yuna Right? Should I make Rudolph his own account, then?

Ing So it'll be a real Catstagram? Is Rudolph going to become a superstar?

Yuna Yeah. Everyone in the world needs to know how cute Rudolph is.

Tips

★**따로** separate

★**본격**
The correct expression is originally 본격적으로 (in earnest).

★**냥스타그램**
An Instagram account or feed where pictures of a cat are uploaded

63

NS

짱

짱 means "really" or "very" and is usually used with an adjective that has positive meaning to emphasize that adjective.

- 너 신발 짱 멋있다. 어디서 샀어?
  Your shoes are super cool. Where did you buy them?

- 오늘 기분 짱 좋다. I'm in a really good mood today.

좋아요 수가 폭발이거든.

폭발 originally means the appearance of power or energy that suddenly spreads or becomes stronger. Therefore if one says 수가 폭발이다, it means that the number of something has suddenly increased.

- 갑자기 조회 수가 폭발이네. 왜 그러지?
  The number of views has suddenly exploded. Why?

- 이번 새 앨범이 인기 폭발이라면서요?
  I heard that the new album is exploding in popularity.

- 이 아이스크림 과일 향이 완전 폭발. This ice cream is bursting with a fruity scent.

N 이/가 폭발이다

64

021

BW

반전 매력

반전 indicates a plot twist, and is usually used a lot in movies or novels. 반전 매력 means an unexpected charm that one gives off when one shows a side that is opposite of their usual appearance.

- 내 최애는 무대에서는 카리스마가 넘치는데 무대 밖에서는 너무 귀여워. 반전 매력 쩔어.
  My bias is overflowing with charisma on stage, but off the stage he's so adorable. His unexpected charm is dope.

- 평소에는 조용해 보였는데 노래방에서 잘 놀더라. 반전 매력이 있는 것 같아.
  She usually seems so quiet, but she plays well at Noraebang. It seems like she has an unexpected charm.

BW

루돌프 귀여운 거 세상 사람들 다 알아야지.

세상 사람들 다 알아야지 is used when one likes something so much that one wishes a lot of people knew about it or they want to tell a lot of people about it. It is also used in the form 세상 사람들 다 알아야 돼.

- 이 집 음식 맛있는 거 세상 사람들 다 알아야지. 내가 인스타에 올려야겠다.
  Everyone in the world should know how delicious the food at this restaurant is. I should upload a post about it to Instagram.

- 내 최애 곡인데 사람들이 잘 몰라서 속상해. 이 노래 좋은 거 사람들이 다 알아야 돼.
  This is my favorite song, but people don't know it well, so I'm upset. Everyone should know how great this song is.

A/V 은/는 거 세상 사람들 다 알아야지.

Using YouTube

Vocabulary

영상 Video

- 유튜브에 영상을 올리다
  to upload a video to YouTube
- 유튜브에서 영상을 보다
  to watch a video on YouTube

자막을 켜고 보다
to watch with subtitles

영상을 재생하다
to play a video

조회수가 잘 나오다
to have a lot of views

유튜브 채널을 개설하다
to set up a YouTube channel

구독 Subscribe

- 유튜브 채널을 구독하다
  to subscribe to a YouTube channel
- 구독자 수가 많다
  to have a lot of subscribers

≡ ▶ UTube   Search   🔍 ⬇

1:01:17 / 3:16:00

👍 1.6만 | 👎 ↗ 공유 ⬇ 오프라인 저장 ⊞ 저장 …

뉴욕에 산다 194만

구독

022

① 유튜브를 하다 to make YouTube videos

나 얼마 전부터 유튜브 해.
Recently, I started making YouTube videos.

② 영상을 촬영하다 to film a video

영상을 촬영을 하긴 했는데 편집이 어려운 것 같아.
I filmed a video, but I think it will be hard to edit it.

③ 브이로그를 찍다 to film a vlog

여행하는 동안 브이로그 한번 찍어 봤어.
I tried filming a vlog while I was traveling.

④ 영상 편집을 하다 to edit a video

영상 편집 쉽게 할 수 있는 앱 좀 추천해 줘.
Please recommend an app so I can easily edit videos.

⑤ 재생 속도를 1.5배로 하고 보다 to watch a video at 1.5x speed

말이 너무 느려서 재생 속도를 1.5배로 하고 봤어.
They speak so slowly, so I watched the video at 1.5x speed.

⑥ 광고를 건너뛰다 to skip an ad

보통은 광고를 건너뛰는데 이 광고는 재미있어서 끝까지 봤어.
I usually skip ads, but this ad was interesting, so I watched it until the end.

⑦ 보다가 말다 to stop watching

내용이 재미없어서 보다가 말았어.
The content was boring, so I stopped watching it.

Dialogue

Tips

★먹방
Short for 먹는 방송(eating broadcast)

Alex   I'm thinking about trying to make YouTube videos.

Hyeonsu   Do you have something in mind?

Alex   Yeah, mukbang. I heard that the profits from ads on successful mukbangs are no joke.

023

Tips

★**엄청** extremely

Hyeonsu	Hey, eating like that might look easy, but not just anyone can do it.
Alex	Should I try a vlog, then? Those also get a lot of views.
Hyeonsu	But do you know how to edit videos?
Alex	Well…. Once I start, I'll figure it out somehow.

뭐 생각해 놓은 거 있어?

This expression is asking if one has a plan or idea. Here, 뭐 is not interrogative; it is short for 뭔가, which indicates something that is not specifically named.

- 생일 선물 사야 하는데 뭐 생각해 놓은 거 있어?
  We have to buy a birthday present. Do you have any ideas?

- 발표 주제 뭐 생각해 놓은 거 있어?
  Do you have something in mind for your presentation?

- A: 이번 주말에 맛있는 음식 만들어 먹을까?
  Shall we try making some delicious food this weekend?

  B: 좋아. 뭐 생각해 놓은 거 있어?
  Sure. Do you have something in mind?

아무나 하는 거 아니다.

This expression means that while it may appear easy at first glance, it's definitely not something everyone can do easily.

- A: 회사 그만두고 카페나 할까? Should I quit my job and open a café?
  B: 그거 아무나 하는 거 아니다. 그냥 회사 열심히 다녀.
  Not just anyone can do that. Just keep working hard at your company.

- 자취는 아무나 하는 게 아니다. Living alone is not for everyone.

- 이번에 배달 아르바이트 해 봤는데 아무나 하는 게 아니더라.
  I tried working a part-time delivery job, but it's not for everyone.

024

어떻게든 되겠지.

This expression is used when one optimistically anticipates that something will progress in some way without specific plans or measures. It can sound irresponsible, so caution should be exercised when using it.

● A: 너 회사 그만뒀다면서? 앞으로 어떻게 할 거야?
   I heard you quit your job. What are you going to do in the future?

   B: 몰라. 어떻게든 되겠지. 지금은 여행이나 다니고 싶어.
   I don't know. It'll work out somehow. I just want to travel right now.

● 외국 생활이 처음이라서 좀 무섭긴 한데, 어떻게든 되겠지요.
   It's my first time living in a foreign country, so I'm a bit scared, but everything will work out somehow.

● A: 너 여행 준비 다 했어?
   Are you ready for your trip?

   B: 그냥 표만 샀어. 가면 어떻게든 되겠지.
   I just bought a ticket. Once I go, I'll figure out the rest.

Quick Check

Using Social Media

■ to use social media   SNS를 [1] 하 다

■ to use Instagram / make YouTube videos   인스타 / 유튜브를 하다

■ to go into Instagram / YouTube   인스타 / 유튜브에 들어가다

Opening an Account

■ to make / open / establish an account   [2] 을 만들다 / 파다 / 개설하다

■ to run an account   계정을 운영하다

■ to make an account public   계정을 공개로 하다

■ to make / turn an account private   계정을 [3] 로 하다 / 돌리다

■ to change one's profile picture   프사를 바꾸다

■ to set up a link to one's profile   프로필에 링크를 걸다

■ to remove / delete one's account   계정을 지우다 / 삭제하다

■ to close one's account   계정을 탈퇴하다

■ to set up a YouTube channel   유튜브 채널을 [4]

1 하다   2 계정   3 비공개   4 개설하다

Adding Friends

- to follow a friend
  친구를 팔로우하다

- to follow each other
  친구와 맞팔하다

- to subscribe to a YouTube channel
  유튜브 채널을 [1] ▨ ▨ ▨ ▨

- to have a lot of followers / subscribers
  팔로워 / 구독자 수가 많다

- to stop following / subscribing ((to) someone's account)
  팔로우 / 구독을 취소하다

- to send a DM to a friend
  친구에게 DM을 보내다

Uploading Posts

- to film a reel
  릴스를 찍다

- to film a video
  영상을 [2] ▨ ▨ ▨ ▨

- to film a vlog
  브이로그를 찍다

- to edit a video
  영상 편집을 하다

- to upload a video to YouTube
  유튜브에 영상을 [3] ▨ ▨ ▨

- to upload a picture / text / feed / post to Instagram
  인스타에 사진 / 글 / 피드 / 게시물을 올리다

---

[1] 구독하다 [2] 촬영하다 [3] 올리다

- new pictures are uploaded to Instagram 인스타에 사진이 새로 올라오다

- one's feed is deleted 피드가 [1] ▢ ▢ ▢

- to hold a live broadcast on Instagram 인스타에서 라이브 방송을 하다

- to do a group purchase on Instagram 인스타로 공구하다

- to tag a friend in a post 게시물에 친구를 태그하다

- to use a cat hashtag 고양이라고 해시태그를 [2] ▢ ▢

Looking at Posts

- to search a hashtag 해시태그를 검색하다

- many ads appear on Instagram 인스타에 광고가 많이 뜨다

- to promote a new product on Instagram 인스타로 새 제품을 홍보하다

- a dance challenge is trending 댄스 챌린지가 유행이다

- to be Instagrammable 인스타 [3] ▢ ▢ ▢

- to be Instagram-worthy 인스타 각이다

- to watch a video on YouTube 유튜브에서 [4] ▢ ▢ 을 보다

1 삭제되다 2 달다 3 감성이다 4 영상

- to play a video — 영상을 재생하다
- to turn on / watch with the subtitles — [1]자막 을 켜고 보다
- to watch a video at 1.5x speed — 재생 속도를 1.5배로 하고 보다
- to skip an ad — 광고를 건너뛰다
- to stop watching — 보다가[2]말다

Reacting to Posts

- to turn on notifications / set up the notification setting — 알림을 켜다 / 알림 설정을 하다
- to turn off notifications / the notification setting — 알림을 끄다 / 알림 설정을 해제하다
- to press "like" on a post — 게시물에 좋아요를[3]누르다
- to have a lot of "likes" on a post — 게시물에 좋아요 수가 많다
- to have a lot of views — [4]조회 수 가 잘 나오다
- to make a good profit from ads — 광고 수익이 좋다
- to leave a comment on a post — 게시물에[5]댓글 을 달다
- to leave a reply to a comment — 댓글에 답글을 남기다
- to save a post — 게시물을 저장하다

1 자막 2 말다 3 누르다 4 조회 수 5 댓글

■ to have a lot of malicious comments on one's feed	피드에 악플이 많이 달리다
■ to report a malicious comment	악플을 신고하다
■ to block an account	계정을 [1]
■ to have one's account blocked by a friend	계정이 친구한테 차단당하다

1 차단하다

3

인터넷만 보면
다 사고 싶어

I Want to Buy Everything
I See on the Internet

1

Online Shopping

Vocabulary

쇼핑몰에 회원 가입하다
to join a store's membership

상품을 인터넷으로/에서 검색하다
to search for a product on the internet

로그인하다 to log in
로그아웃하다 to log out

제품을 찜하다
to add a product to one's
wishlist / favorites

색상을 선택하다
to select a color

상품평 / 리뷰를 확인하다
to check the product ratings / reviews

물건을 장바구니에 담아 놓다
to put an item in one's cart

025

1 **신상이 나오다** a new product is released

A: 너 운동화 샀어?
  Did you buy sneakers?
B: 조금 기다렸다가 신상이 나오면 사려고.
  I'm going to wait a bit and buy them when the new model is released.

2 **가격을 비교해서 최저가를 확인하다**
to compare prices and check the lowest price

A: 선풍기 하나 사야겠다.
  I should buy an electric fan.
B: 먼저 가격을 비교해서 최저가 확인해 봐.
  First, compare prices and check how much the lowest price is.

3 **이 사이트에는 초특가로 상품이 나오다**
this website releases products at special prices

A: 와, 이 사이트에는 초특가로 상품이 나왔네.
  Wow, this site releases products at special prices.
B: 그러게, 엄청 싸다. 여기서 주문하자.
  Yeah, they're really cheap. Let's order from here.

4 **마음에 드는 물건을 찜해 놓다**
to add an item that one likes to one's wishlist / favorites

A: 세일 기간에 사려고 마음에 드는 물건을 찜해 놨어.
  I added the item I like to my wishlist so I can buy it when it goes on sale.
B: 맞아. 세일 안 할 때 사는 건 왠지 좀 아까워.
  Right. Buying something when it's not on sale feels like a bit of a waste, for some reason.

Dialogue

Tips

*니
Informal expression of 네(your)

Mael   Look at this bag. I put it in my cart a few weeks ago. Should I buy it or not?

Ing   It's pretty. It's totally your style.

Mael   Right? But it's so expensive that I've been going back and forth about it for weeks.

Ing   Did you try comparing prices again? Usually the lowest price keeps changing.

026

> **Tips**
>
> ★지르다
> Slang for 사다(to buy)

Mael	Oh! This site actually gives a discount coupon.
Ing	It's way cheaper, then. Stop agonizing about it and just buy it.
Mael	Yeah, I've worked really hard lately, so I deserve this.
Ing	Hurry and buy it so you can use it more often.

이거 살까 말까?

이거 살까 말까? is short for 이거 살까? 사지 말까? and is used when one is debating whether to buy something or not. V을까 말까? is an expression used when asking others for advice about whether to do something or not, and when one is worried about which choice would be best.

- 이미 한 잔 마셨는데 한 잔 더 마실까 말까?
  I already drank one glass. Should I drink another one or not?

- 다음 주에 시험인데, 주말에 팬 미팅이 있어. 갈까 말까?
  Exams are next week, but there's a fan meeting this weekend. Should I go or not?

- 사실은, 이거 비밀인데 말할까 말까?
  To be honest, this is a secret, so I'm not sure if I should say it or not.

V 을까 말까?

몇 주째 고민만 하고 있어.

This expression can be used when one has been pondering for weeks without taking any action. N만 V고 있다 is used when one remains in a situation for a long time without proceeding with the subsequent action that should follow. It can be used with expressions like 몇 주째, 며칠 째, 몇 시간 째, 몇 분 째, and so on.

- 쟤는 숙제는 안 하고 몇 시간째 게임만 하고 있어.
  He's not doing his homework and just has been playing video games for hours.

- 내 동생은 약속에 늦었는데도 출발하지 않고 몇 분째 지도 앱만 보고 있어.
  My younger brother is late for his appointment, but he hasn't left and has just been looking at the map app for several minutes.

- 몇 달째 한글만 배우는 중. I've only been learning Hangeul for a few months.

몇 주째 **N** 만 **V** 고 있다

027

NS

열일

This is a coinage wherein 열심히 and 일하다 are combined and used in phrases like 열일 or 열일하다. A similar coinage is 열공, which combines 열심히 and 공부하다.

- **다음 달부터 열일해야 돼.** Starting next month, I have to work hard.

- **시험이라 주말 내내 열공.** I have an exam, so I'm studying hard all weekend.

BW

빨리 사서 자주 하고 다니는 게 남는 거야.

자주 하고 다니다 means "to use something a lot," and 남다 means it is profitable. Therefore, the above sentence means that if one is in a situation where you are debating whether to buy something or not, and you are going to buy it anyway, you should not hesitate—you should buy it quickly and use it often because it will be beneficial. So, this expression is urging the other person to buy the item quickly.

A: 이어폰이 하나 필요한데 지금 살까? 나중에 신상 나오면 그때 살까?
  I need earphones, but should I buy them now? Or should I buy them later when a new model comes out?

B: 하루라도 빨리 사서 자주 하고 다니는 게 남는 거야. 얼른 사.
  You should just buy them quickly so you can get a lot of use out of them. Hurry and buy them.

2

Purchasing

Vocabulary

상품을 20% 할인하다
a product is discounted by 20%

배송비가 무료다
shipping is free

무통장 입금
Deposit without a Bankbook

현금으로 결제하다
to pay with cash

계좌 이체를 하다
to make a bank transfer

카드 결제
Credit Card Payment

카드로 결제하다
to pay by credit card

일시불로 하다
to pay all at once

3개월 할부로 하다
to pay across 3 months

3개월 무이자 할부가 되다
a payment is split across
3 months without interest

포인트가 적립되다
to earn points

① 상품을 사다 / 구매하다 to buy / purchase a product

포인트를 사용해서 상품을 구매했어요.
I used points to buy a product.

② 상품을 주문하다 to order a product

상품을 주문하고 3일 후에 받았어요.
I ordered a product and received it 3 days later.

③ 충동구매를 하다 to buy on impulse

필요한 게 아닌데 세일해서 충동구매를 한 것 같아.
It's not something I need, but I think I bought it on impulse because it was on sale.

④ 쿠폰을 적용해서 할인을 받다 to apply a coupon and receive a discount

생일 쿠폰을 적용해서 2만 원 할인을 받았어.
I used my birthday coupon and received a 20,000 won discount.

⑤ 할인을 받아서 사다 to buy something at a discount

할인을 받아서 2만 원쯤 싸게 샀어.
I received a discount and bought it for about 20,000 won less.

⑥ 배송지를 입력하다 to enter one's delivery address

실수로 배송지를 잘못 입력해서 택배가 다른 곳으로 갔어요.
I incorrectly entered my delivery address on accident, so the package went to the wrong place.

Dialogue

Mael   Yuna, aren't you a member of this site?

Yuna   Yeah, I buy almost everything from here.

Mael   I'm going to buy a bag from this site, but it says that VIP customers get up to 20% off.

Yuna   Really? I'm probably a VIP.

Mael   Can you order it for me using your ID?

Yuna   Sure, let me know the model name.

Yuna   Is this the right one? I'll order it. How do you want to pay?

Mael   Please pay it all at once with your credit card. I'll transfer the money to your bank account.

회원이지 않아?

회원이야? is used when one simply asks someone whether they are a member or not, but 회원이지 않아? is used when the speaker knows that the other person is a member and wants to confirm it. N이지 않아? is an expression used to casually confirm what you already know.

- **내일이 료 생일이지 않아?** Isn't tomorrow Ryo's birthday?

- **니 친구 서울대학교 학생이지 않아?**
  Isn't your friend a student at Seoul National University?

- **너 다음 주에 휴가지 않아?** Aren't you off from work next week?

N 이지 않아?

VIP 등급일걸?

VIP 등급일걸? is an expression used when one is not completely sure, but one is guessing that they are a VIP. A/V을걸? carries a relatively strong confidence in the guess, but is used to avoid a definitive feeling. And should be said with a raised tone at the end.

- **여기는 항상 최저가로 팔아서 제일 쌀걸?**
  This place always sells at the lowest price, so it's probably the cheapest.

- **주말이라 백화점에 사람들이 많을걸?**
  It's the weekend, so there are probably a lot of people at the department store.

- **그건 이미 가지고 있을걸? 다른 선물 사 주자.**
  I think she already has that. Let's buy her a different present.

A/V 을걸?

030

주문해 주면 안 돼?

Similar to 주문해 줘, this expression is used when asking someone to order something. If one uses V아/어 주면 안 돼? to ask favor, it conveys a more earnest and softer feeling than the command form V아/어 줘.

- **생일 선물로 이거 사 주면 안 돼?** Could you buy this for me as a birthday present?

- **대중교통으로 가기 힘든데 니가 운전해 주면 안 돼?**
  It's difficult to get there using public transportation. Can't you drive me there?

- **한국어를 배워 볼까 하는데 니가 좀 가르쳐 주면 안 돼?**
  I'm thinking about trying to learn Korean. Could you teach me?

V 아/어 주면 안 돼?

3

Making an Inquiry

Vocabulary

배송 날짜를 10월 13일로 지정하다
to set the delivery date to October 13th

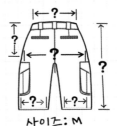

사이즈: M

상세 사이즈가 안 나와 있다
the detailed size is not provided

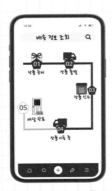

앱에서/으로 배송 정보를 조회하다
to view the shipping information via an app

송장 번호를 확인하다
to check an invoice number

배송지를 변경하다
to change one's delivery address

택배가 안 오다
the delivery did not arrive

031

① 배송이 늦어지다 / 지연되다 delivery is delayed

배송이 늦어져서 죄송합니다.
We apologize that your delivery has been delayed.

② 물건이 아직 배송 중이다 an item is still being shipped

지난주에 주문했는데 물건이 아직 배송 중이네요.
I ordered the item last week, but it's still being shipped.

③ 주문이 많이 밀려 있다 orders are very backed up

주문이 많이 밀려 있어서 배송이 지연되고 있습니다.
Orders are very backed up, so shipments are being delayed.

④ 까만색이 품절되다 black is sold out

죄송하지만 까만색은 품절됐어요.
We're sorry, but this item is sold out in black.

⑤ 물품이 재입고되다 a product is restocked

물품이 재입고되면 안내해 드리겠습니다.
We will let you know when the product is restocked.

⑥ 사이즈가 크게 나오다 the size runs large

이 옷은 사이즈가 크게 나왔어요. 한 사이즈 작게 주문해 주세요.
The size of this clothing item runs large. Please order one size smaller than usual.

Dialogue

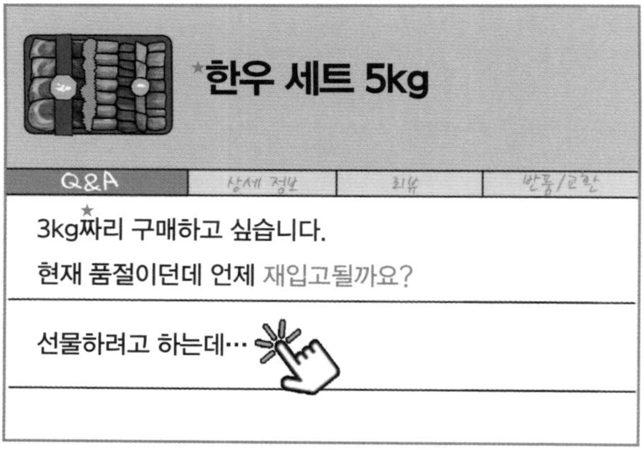
★한우 세트 5kg
Q&A
상세 정보
리뷰
반품/교환
3kg★짜리 구매하고 싶습니다.
현재 품절이던데 언제 재입고될까요?
선물하려고 하는데…

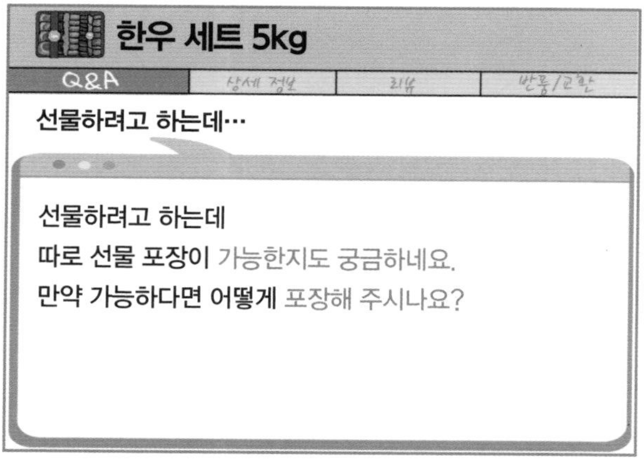
한우 세트 5kg
Q&A
상세 정보
리뷰
반품/교환
선물하려고 하는데…
선물하려고 하는데
따로 선물 포장이 가능한지도 궁금하네요.
만약 가능하다면 어떻게 포장해 주시나요?

Tips

★**한우 세트** Korean beef gift set
★**짜리** worth, amount

5kg Korean Beef Gift Set

▶ I want to buy 3kg set. It's currently sold out; when will it be restocked?
▶ I would like to buy this as a gift…

▶ I would like to buy this as a gift…
I would like to buy this as a gift, so I'd like to know if gift wrapping is possible.
If it is possible, how is it wrapped?

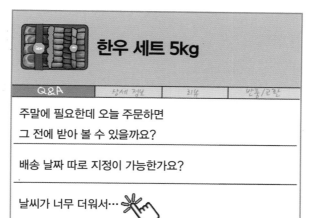

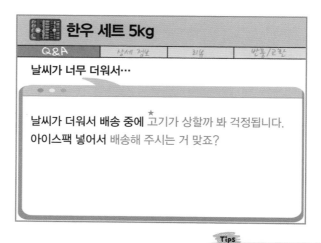

032

Tips

★**고기가 상하다** for meat to spoil

▶ I need it this weekend. If I order today, will I be able to receive it before then?
▶ Is it possible to set the delivery date?
▶ The weather is hot, so …

▶ The weatehr is hot, so …
The weatehr is hot, so I'm worried that the meat will spoil during shipment.
It's packed in ice before being shipped, right?

재입고 될까요?
가능한지도 궁금하네요.
포장해 주시나요?

The sentence endings A/V을까요?, A/V은/는지 궁금하다, A/V나요/은가요? are often used while making an inquiry with a courteous and polite tone. A/V은/는지 궁금하다 is used to express inquiries in a roundabout way, while "A/V나요/은가요?" has a gentler tone.

● 배송 날짜를 지정할 수 있을까요? Would I be able to set the delivery date?

● 어떻게 포장해 주시는지 궁금해요. I'm wondering how it's packaged.

● 언제 재입고되나요? When will it be restocked?

A/V 을까요?
A/V 은/는지 궁금하다
A/V 나요/은가요?

033

고기가 상할까 봐 걱정됩니다.

This expression means that one is worried that the meat may spoil. When one is worried about something bad that might happen, A/V을까 봐 걱정되다 is used.

- **물건이 배송 중에 깨질까 봐 걱정돼요.**
  I'm worried that the item will break while being shipped.

- **내일까지 물건을 못 받을까 봐 걱정되네요.**
  I'm worried that I won't be able to receive the item by tomorrow.

- **사이즈가 안 맞을까 봐 걱정되는데, 사이즈 좀 자세히 알려 주실래요?** I'm worried that the size won't be right. Could you provide more details about the sizing?

A/V 을까 봐 걱정되다

배송해 주시는 거 맞죠?

A/V은/는 거 맞죠? is used when one wants to remind the other person of their request or to confirm a fact they already know.

- **이거 두 개 사면 한 개 더 보내 주는 거 맞죠?**
  If I buy two of these, I get another one free, right?

- **어제 주문했는데, 이번 주까지 도착하는 거 맞죠?**
  I ordered it yesterday. It will arrive this week, right?

- **열 시에 문 여는 거 맞죠?** It opens at 10:00, right?

A/V 은/는 거 맞죠?

Issues and Returning

Vocabulary

제품이 잘못 오다
the wrong product arrived

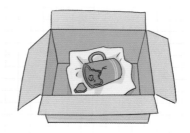

제품이 깨져서 오다
the product arrived broken

반품 / 교환을 신청하다
to request a return / exchange

S 사이즈를 M 사이즈로 교환하다
to exchange a size S for a size M

택배 기사가 물품을 수거하다
the delivery driver collects the item

제품을 환불 받다
to receive a refund for a product

034

1 **주문 내역을 확인하다** to confirm the order details

결제하기 전에 한 번 더 주문 내역을 확인했어요.
Before paying, I confirmed the order details one more time.

2 **다른 사람이 쓰던 제품 같다** to seem like an item used by someone else

이거 다른 사람이 쓰던 제품 같아요. 화장품이 묻어 있어요. 새 제품으로 교환해 주세요.
This seems like an item that was used by someone else. There are makeup stains on it.
Please exchange it for a new item.

3 **불량이 오다** for a defective product to arrive

불량이 왔어요. 작동이 안 돼요.
A defective product has arrived. It doesn't work.

4 **왕복 배송비를 부담하다** to be responsible for return shipping costs

다른 색상으로 교환하려면 왕복 배송비를 부담하셔야 해요.
If you would like to exchange it for a different color, you are responsible for the return
shipping fees.

5 **반품 / 교환 신청을 취소하다** to cancel a return / exchange request

왕복 배송비를 부담하라고 해서 반품 신청을 취소했어.
They said I would have to pay for return shipping, so I canceled my return request.

6 **환불까지 7일이 걸리다** it takes 7 days to receive a refund

오늘 반품을 신청하면 환불까지 7일이 걸립니다.
If you request a return today, it will take 7 days for the refund to be completed.

Dialogue

Tips

★ **일단** first, for now

★ **색깔이 튀다** for a color to stand out

Alex   Huh? What's this? Did I order a red one?

Hyeonsu   What's wrong? Did you get the wrong item?

Alex   I'm pretty sure I ordered a white one, but I received a red one.

Hyeonsu   The design is pretty good. Just try it on first.

Alex   No, the color is too bold for me to wear it. Do you want it?

035

Hyeonsu I'm good. Just get a refund.

Alex I ordered a white t-shirt, but I received a red one. I'd like to get a refund. What do I need to do?

Shopping Mall Employee I'll check your order details.

Shopping Mall Employee I'm so sorry. There was a mistake on our end. I'll initiate a refund immediately

나도 됐다.

됐다 is an expression of refusal when one is offered something. It does not feel friendly or kind; rather, it is assertive. Therefore, it is mainly used between people who are close and comfortable with each other. To politely refuse an offer, it is good to use the expressions like 괜찮아요, 아니에요.

- A: 커피 마실래? Want some coffee?
  B: 나는 괜찮아. 안 마실래. I'm okay. I don't want any.
  C: 나도 됐어. Me either.

- A: 너도 같이 쇼핑 가자. You should come shopping with us, too.
  B: 나는 됐어. I'm good.

- A: 내가 좀 도와줄까? Want me to help you?
  B: 됐어. 너는 그냥 쉬어. That's okay. You just rest.

N 은/는 됐다.

환불 받고 싶은데 어떻게 하면 돼요?

어떻게 하면 돼요? is an expression that is used when one does not know a certain method or process, and would like to receive guidance. A/V은/는데 can be used in the front part of the sentence to explain one's situation.

- 상품을 잘못 선택해서 다시 주문하려고 하는데 어떻게 하면 돼요?
  I chose the wrong item, so I'd like to submit another order. What do I need to do?

- 배송지를 변경하고 싶은데 어떻게 하면 돼요?
  I want to change my delivery address. How can I do that?

- 와이파이 연결이 안 되는데 어떻게 하면 돼요?
  The wi-fi won't connect. What should I do?

A/V 은/는데 어떻게 하면 돼요?

036

죄송해서 어쩌죠?

죄송해서 어쩌죠? is a friendly way of saying to express the feeling of being so sorry that you don't know what to do. A similar expression is 죄송해서 어떡하죠?

- **죄송해서 어쩌죠? 쿠키가 다 팔렸어요.** I'm so sorry. The cookies have all been sold.

- **A: 오늘 일곱 시에 네 명 예약했어요.** I made a reservation for four people at 7:00.

  B: 죄송해서 어쩌죠? 아직 테이블 정리가 안 끝났어요. 얼른 정리하고 안내해 드릴게요.
  I'm so sorry. The table isn't ready yet. We'll quickly arrange it and let you know when it's ready.

- **미안해서 어떡하지? 나 30분쯤 늦을 것 같아.**
  I'm so sorry. I think I'll be about 30 minutes late.

저희 측

측 means the side that is opposite to another side, and is used to refer to a certain side or group involved in a conversation. 저희 측 is a more humble way to express 우리 측, and when used as a subject in the sentence, 에서 used as a subject particle instead of 이/가.

- **저희 측 실수로 불편을 드려 죄송합니다.**
  We are sorry that a mistake on our end caused you discomfort.

- **물건을 아직 못 받으셨다고요? 저희 측에서 확인해 보고 연락 드릴게요.**
  You still haven't received the item? We will check on our end and contact you.

Quick Check

Shopping Mall Membership

■	to join a store's membership	쇼핑몰에 회원 가입하다
■	to log in	로그인하다
■	to log out	로그아웃하다

Searching for a Product

■	to search for a product on the internet	상품을 인터넷으로/에서 검색하다
■	a new product is released	신상이 [1] 나 오 다
■	to compare prices and check the lowest price	가격을 비교해서 [2] ▢▢▢를 확인하다
■	this website releases products at special prices	이 사이트에는 초특가로 상품이 나오다
■	to check the product ratings / reviews	상품평 / 리뷰를 확인하다

Ordering

■	to add a product to one's wishlist / favorites	제품을 [3] ▢▢▢

1 나오다   2 최저가   3 찜하다

■ to add an item that one likes to one's wishlist / favorites	마음에 드는 물건을 찜해 놓다
■ to select a size / quantity / color	사이즈 / 수량 / 색상을 선택하다
■ to put an item in one's cart	물건을 장바구니에 [1]◻◻ ◻◻
■ to buy / purchase a product	상품을 사다 / 구매하다
■ to order a product	상품을 주문하다
■ to buy on impulse	충동구매를 하다
■ to confirm the order details	주문 내역을 확인하다

Payment

■ to pay by credit card	카드로 [2]◻◻◻◻
■ to pay all at once	[3]◻◻◻ 로 하다
■ to pay across 3 months	3개월 [4]◻◻◻ ◻◻
■ a payment is split across 3 months without interest	3개월 무이자 할부가 되다
■ deposit without a bankbook	무통장 입금
■ to pay with cash	현금으로 결제하다
■ to make a bank transfer	계좌 이체를 하다

1 담아 놓다 2 결제하다 3 일시불 4 할부로 하다

■ to earn points	포인트가[1] ▦ ▦ ▦
■ a product is discounted by 20%	상품을 20%[2] ▦ ▦ ▦
■ to apply a coupon and receive a discount	쿠폰을 적용해서 할인을 받다
■ to buy something at a discount	할인을 받아서 사다

Delivery

■ shipping is free	배송비가[3] ▦ ▦ ▦
■ to be responsible for return shipping costs	왕복 배송비를[4] ▦ ▦ ▦
■ to enter one's delivery address	배송지를 입력하다
■ to change one's delivery address	배송지를 변경하다
■ to set the delivery date to October 13th	배송 날짜를 10월 13일로 지정하다
■ to view the shipping information via an app	앱에서/으로 배송 정보를 조회하다
■ delivery is delayed	배송이 늦어지다 / [5] ▦ ▦ ▦
■ an item is still being shipped	물건이 아직[6] ▦ ▦ 이다

1 적립되다 2 할인하다 3 무료다 4 부담하다 5 지연되다 6 배송 중

Inquiries and Requests

- to check an invoice number — 송장 번호를 확인하다
- the delivery did not arrive — 택배가 안 오다
- orders are very backed up — 주문이 많이 [1] ▩ ▩ ▩ ▩
- a product is restocked — 물품이 [2] ▩ ▩ ▩ ▩ ▩
- the detailed size is not provided — 상세 사이즈가 안 나와 있다
- the size runs large — 사이즈가 크게 나오다
- black is sold out — 까만색이 [3] ▩ ▩ ▩ ▩

Reason for Refund

- the wrong product arrived — 제품이 [4] ▩ ▩ ▩ ▩
- the product arrived broken — 제품이 깨져서 오다
- to seem like an item used by someone else — 다른 사람이 쓰던 제품 같다
- for a defective product to arrive — 불량이 오다

Returns and Exchanges

- to request a return / exchange — 반품 / 교환을 [5] ▩ ▩ ▩ ▩

1 밀려 있다 2 재입고되다 3 품절되다 4 잘못 오다 5 신청하다

■ to exchange a size S for a size M   S사이즈를 M사이즈로 교환하다

■ to receive a refund for a product   제품을 [1]

■ it takes 7 days to receive
a refund   환불까지 7일이 걸리다

■ the delivery driver collects
the item   택배 기사가 물품을 수거하다

■ to cancel a return /
exchange request   반품 / 교환 신청을 취소하다

1 환불 받다

4

오늘은 하루 종일 넷플릭스

Today, I'm Watching Netflix
All Day Long

Selecting Content

Vocabulary

넷플릭스에 새 시리즈가 나오다
a new series is released on Netflix

드라마에 민시아가
나오다 / 출연하다
Min Si-ah appears in the drama

한번에
몰아서 보다
to watch all at once

아직 결말이 안 나다
the conclusion has not been
released yet

최종화가 올라오다
the final episode comes out

시즌 2가 3월에 공개되다
season 2 will be released in March

① **넷플릭스에 가입하다** to join Netflix

넷플릭스에 가입한 후 매일 두 시간씩 드라마를 봐.
After joining Netflix, I watch TV shows for two hours every day.

② **한 달 무료 체험을 하다** to try 1 month for free

가입하기 전에 한 달 무료 체험 먼저 해 봐.
Before joining, try 1 month for free first.

③ **가족과 계정을 공유하다** to share an account with one's family

언니랑 넷플릭스 계정을 공유하고 요금은 반반씩 내고 있어.
I share a Netflix account with my older sister, and we each pay half the cost.

④ **뭐 볼지 고르다** to choose what to watch

A: 뭐 볼지 골랐어?
  Did you choose what to watch?

B: 글쎄, 너는 보고 싶은 거 있어?
  I'm not sure. Is there something you want to watch?

⑤ **민시아가 주인공을 맡다** Min Si-ah plays the main character

민시아가 주인공 맡은 영화, 그거 재미있대.
I heard that the movie with Min Si-ah playing the main character is fun.

⑥ **이 예능이 반응이 좋다** this variety show has a good response

요즘 이 예능이 반응이 좋다는데 이거 볼래?
This variety show has a good response these days. Want to watch this?

⑦ **정주행하다** to watch from start to finish

바빠서 못 봤던 드라마를 주말 동안 다 정주행했어.
I've been too busy to watch this drama, so over the weekend I watched the whole thing from start to finish.

Dialogue

Ryo	Shall I stay at home all weekend and watch a drama?
Ryo	Is there anything that would be good to watch these days?
Hyeonsu	You should watch "The Villains." From the first episode, the immersiveness is no joke.
Ryo	Really? Who's in it?
Hyeonsu	There aren't any famous actors in it. But recently, it's really freaking popular.

Tips

★**몰입감** immersiveness

Ryo	Then I guess I should watch it. I should watch it all at once this weekend.
Hyeonsu	But it's not done yet. The final episode hasn't been released.
Ryo	What, seriously? Then I'll save it to my watch list and watch it once all the episodes are out.

NS

집콕

집콕 is a new word derived from the phrase 집에만 콕 박혀 있다, meaning to stay inside and not come out of one's house. It can be used in the form of 집콕 or 집콕하다. A similar expression is 방콕하다, which means to stay inside one's room.

● **어제 집콕하면서 유튜브만 봤어.**
  Yesterday, I stayed at home and just watched YouTube.

● **주말인데 너무 추워서 집콕하려고.**
  It's the weekend, but it's so cold that I'm going to just stay in my house.

● **A: 너 지금 뭐 해?** What are you doing right now?
  B: 그냥 집콕 중인데. I'm just staying at home.

볼 만한 거 뭐 있어?

V을 만한 거 뭐 있어? is an expression used when someone wants to receive a recommendation, typically for something decent and satisfactory.

● **좀 가볍게 먹고 싶은데 먹을 만한 거 뭐가 있지?**
  I want to eat something light. What do we have that would be good to eat?

● **여기 커피 말고 마실 만한 거 뭐 있어?**
  Is there anything good to drink here besides coffee?

● **노트북 쓸 만한 거 뭐 있어?**
  What kind of laptop is good to use?

V을 만한 거 뭐 있어?

에이, 뭐야?

This is an expression that conveys disappointment in something one expected or feeling dumbfounded by an absurd event. However, depending on the intonation, a variety of emotions can be expressed, such as surprise or being moved as well as being irritated.

● 에이, 뭐야? 오늘인 줄 알았는데 내일이잖아.
Seriously? I thought it was today, but it's tomorrow.

● A: 미안, 나 갑자기 일이 생겨서 못 갈 것 같아.
Sorry, something suddenly came up, so I don't think I can go.

B: 에이, 뭐야? 일부러 너희 회사 근처로 예약한 건데······.
Are you serious? I intentionally made a reservation at a place close to your office···.

● A: 생일 축하해.
Happy birthday.

B: 에이, 뭐야? 오늘 못 온다고 했잖아.
What the heck? You said you couldn't come today.

2

Watching Content

Vocabulary

소리를 키우다
to turn up the volume

소리를 줄이다
to turn down the volume

밝기를 조절하다
to adjust the brightness

건너뛰면서 보다
to skip

재생 버튼을 누르다
to press the play button

앞으로 돌려서 보다
to rewind

정지 버튼을 누르다
to press the pause button

영화를 2배 속으로 보다
to watch a movie at 2x speed

음성을 원어로 설정하다
to set the audio to the original language

자막을 한국어로 설정하다
to set the subtitles to Korean

① 드라마를 보다 / 시청하다
to watch a drama

이번 주말에는 집에서 드라마나 봐야지.
I should watch a drama at home this weekend.

② 한국 영화를 영어 더빙으로 보다
to watch a Korean movie with English dubbing

자막을 읽는 게 귀찮아서 한국 영화를 영어 더빙으로 봤어요.
It's bothersome to read subtitles, so I watched a Korean movie with English dubbing.

③ 영화를 다운받다 / 저장하다
to download / save a movie

비행기에서 보려고 미리 영화를 다운받았어요.
I downloaded the movie in advance to watch it on the airplane.

④ 잠깐 멈추다
to pause for a moment

잠깐 멈춰 봐. 화장실 좀 갔다 올게.
Pause it for a moment. I'm going to go to the bathroom.

⑤ 잠깐 멈췄다가 이어서 보다
to continue watching after momentarily pausing

중요한 전화가 왔는데 잠깐 멈췄다가 이어서 보자.
A crucial phone call came in, so let's pause for a bit and then continue watching.

⑥ 꼼짝도 안 하고 넷플릭스만 보다
to not move a muscle and only watch Netflix

주말에 꼼짝도 안 하고 침대에 누워서 넷플릭스만 봤어.
Over the weekend, I didn't move a muscle and just laid in bed and watched Netflix.

Dialogue

Yuna   Come here and take a seat.

Mael   What did the male lead say? I couldn't hear him.

Yuna   I didn't hear him, either.

Tips

★남주

Short for 남자 주인공(main male character). 여자 주인공 (main female character) is shortened to 여주.

041

Mael   Then shall we rewind it a bit and watch it again?

Yuna   Yeah, and turn up the volume a little.

Mael   Agh, what did he say? I couldn't hear him again. Even though we turned up the volume, I have no idea what he's saying.

Yuna   He mumbles too much.

Mael   I think it'd be better to watch with subtitles.

남주가 뭐래? / 뭐라는 거야?

When one is unable to hear what the main male character says and asks the person watching with them what he said, 남주가 뭐래? / 뭐라는 거야? is used. When you have trouble hearing what was said due to surrounding noise, the speaker's pronunciation, the volume of the speaker's voice, or the speaker's talking speed, this expression is used to ask other people who are present at the same time about the content of the speech. However, depending on the intonation, it can give a mixed feeling of irritation, so one must be careful.

- 저 직원 목소리가 너무 작네. 뭐래?
  That employee's voice is so quiet. What did he say?

- 마이크 소리가 잘 안 들리는데 진행자가 뭐래?
  I can't hear what he's saying into the microphone. What did the host say?

- 저 배우 발음이 너무 안 좋은데 뭐라는 거야?
  That actor has terrible pronunciation. What did he say?

N 이/가 뭐래? / 뭐라는 거야?

못 알아듣겠어.

못 알아듣겠어 means that even if you hear what someone say, you cannot understand what they mean. When 못 and V겠어 are used together, it means that you can't do something even if you try. It can only be used when a first-person speaker is talking about his/her situation.

- 지갑이 어디 있는지 못 찾겠어. I have no idea where my wallet is.

042

● 진짜 재미없다. 끝까지 보려고 했는데 다 못 보겠어.
This is so boring. I was going to watch it to the end, but I can't do it.

● 다리가 너무 아파서 못 걷겠어. My legs hurt too much to walk.

못 V 겠다

아무래도 자막 켜고 보는 게 낫겠다.

This sentence means that the speaker tried a variety of ways to hear the sound better, such as turning up the volume, but it didn't work; so, in conclusion, it would be better to watch it with the subtitles turned on. 아무래도 means "though one should think about, or try this or that." The expression 아무래도 V는 게 낫겠다 is used when reaching a conclusion regarding what to do next after thinking and trying various things. Consent may also be sought by using the form V는 게 낫겠지?

● 아무래도 다음에 만나는 게 낫겠다.
In any case, I think it'd be better if we meet next time.

● 아무래도 안 가는 게 낫겠다. It would be better not to go.

● 아무래도 오늘 끝내는 게 낫겠지?
In any case, it would be best to finish it today, right?

아무래도 V 는 게 낫겠다

3

Evaluating Content

Vocabulary

주연이 연기를 잘하다
the main actor is good at acting

거기 서!

조연이 딕션이 좋다
the supporting actor has good diction

감독의 연출이 좋다
the director's directing ability is good

이 영화는 실화를 바탕으로...

실화라서 소름 돋다
to get goosebumps because it's a true story

The end

결말이 어이없다
the ending is absurd

영상미가 뛰어나다
the visual beauty is outstanding

① 시나리오가 탄탄하다 the screenplay is solid

시나리오가 탄탄해서 몰입감이 좋았어요.
The screenplay was solid, so the sense of immersiveness was good.

② 반전이 충격적이다 the plot twist is shocking

마지막에 반전이 정말 충격적임.
The plot twist at the end is really shocking.

③ 스토리가 허술하다 the story is weak

액션은 화려하나 스토리는 너무나 허술합니다.
The action is impressive, but the story is very weak.

④ 스토리를 질질 끌다 the story is dragged out

중반부터 스토리를 질질 끌어서 좀 지루했어.
From the middle of the movie, the story was dragged out and was a bit boring.

⑤ 스토리가 진부하다 the story is cliché

스토리는 좀 진부했지만 배우들 연기만큼은 최고였어요.
The story was a bit cliché, but the actors' acting was the best.

⑥ 이 영화는 호불호가 엇갈리다

this movie has a mix of positive and negative reviews

이 영화는 잔인한 장면 때문에 호불호가 엇갈리는 것 같아요.
This film seems to have a mix of positive and negative reviews because of the cruel scenes.

⑦ 시간이 아깝다 to be a waste of time

혹시나 해서 끝까지 봤는데 시간이 아까웠어.
I watched until the end just in case it got better, but it was a waste of time.

⑧ 소설을 원작으로 하다 to be based on a novel

이 드라마는 소설을 원작으로 해서 소설과 비교하면서 보는 재미가 있네요.
This drama is based on a novel, so it's fun to watch it while comparing it to the novel.

Dialogue

시청 후기

▼ 높은 평가 순

★★★★★
제발 이 드라마 안 본 사람들 없게 해 주세요. 🥹❤️
👍 232 💬 80

★★★★★
시나리오, 연기, 연출, 그냥 다 미쳤음.★
하루 만에★ 정주행해 버림.
👍 145 💬 38

★★★★★
주연부터 조연까지 어느 한 명 연기 구멍이 없음. 😌👍
👍 82 💬 26

★★★★★
마지막에 반전이 충격적이었다. 😱
👍 67 💬 4

▶ Please make sure there are no people who haven't watched this drama.

▶ The screenplay, acting, directing, it's all just insane. I ended up watching the whole thing in one day.

▶ From the lead actors to the supporting roles, not a single person has any flaws in their acting.

▶ The plot twist at the end was shocking.

Tips

★(미쳤)음
–음 is an ending that combines with a verb or an adjective to form a noun. Recently, it has mainly been used when leaving short online posts of one or two sentences, such as reviews, KakaoTalk conversations, and Instagram posts.

★하루 만에 in one day

044

시청 후기

▼ 높은 평가 순

★ ★

결말이 궁금해서 중간중간 건너뛰면서 겨우겨우 봤음.

👍 32 💬 18

★

이런 어이없는 결말은 진짜 역대급.

👍 14 💬 3

★

인생 최악의 두 시간. 아까운 내 두 시간. 👎😫

👍 8 💬 1

Tips

★**중간중간** (to skip) here and there (in a film/show)
★**겨우겨우** barely, with great difficulty

▶ I was curious about the ending, so I barely watched it while skipping through it.

▶ This is truly the most ridiculous ending of all time.

▶ It was the worst two hours of my life. It was a waste of my two hours.

BW

제발 이 드라마 안 본 사람들 없게 해 주세요.

This implies a hope that there isn't anyone who hasn't watched this drama. 안 V아/어 본 사람들 없게 해 주세요 is an expression used when actively recommending something on the internet, expressing a desire for everyone to try and experience it because it is so great.

- 제발 이 영화 안 본 사람들 없게 해 주세요.
  Please make sure that there are no people who haven't seen this movie.

- 제발 이 식당 안 가 본 사람 없게 해 주세요.
  Please make sure that there are no people who haven't gone to this restaurant.

- 이 펜 안 써 본 사람 없게 해 주세요. Everyone should really use this pen.

제발 이 **N** 안 **V**아/어 본 사람들 없게 해 주세요.

BW **IL**

미쳤음

Literally, 미쳤다 means "crazy", or "insane", but it became a new expression used to say something is the best, really good, or outstanding. It implies that the level, quality, and ability are so excellent that it's far beyond what an average person can achieve in normal circumstances.

- 이번 노래 완전 미쳤다. 너무 좋음. This song is totally insane. It's so good.

- 저 사람 춤 추는 거 봐. 미쳤네. Look at that person dancing. That's wild.

- 한국 인터넷 속도 미쳤음. Korean internet speeds are crazy.

N 이/가 미쳤다

045

BW

구멍이 없음

구멍 literally means "a hole", but in this expression means, a loophole, weakness, shortcoming, or a person with such weaknesses. 구멍이 없다 means that everything is good, with nothing lacking or falling behind. It is used not only to individuals but also to evaluate dramas, movies, idol groups, sports teams, etc., where multiple people work together as a team.

- 모든 멤버가 마음에 드는 그룹은 처음. 구멍이 없네.
  This is the first band that I like all of the members. All of the members are great.
- 이 드라마는 연기 구멍이 한 명도 없어.
  This drama doesn't have a single weak actor in it.
- 저 농구 선수한테는 구멍이 없어. 역대급으로 완벽한 선수야.
  That basketball player has no weaknesses. He's the most perfect player of all time.

N 에/에게 구멍이 없다

NS

역대급

역대급 is a new word that combines 역대, which refers to the time that has been passed down from generation to generation, and 급, which refers to level. It is not a grammatically correct expression, but it is often used in daily life, newspapers, broadcast, etc. to mean that something is the best or worst that has ever existed. It is also used in the forms 역대급이다, 역대급으로.

- 이번에 새로 나온 핸드폰 봤어? 완전 역대급이던데?
  Did you see the new phone that just came out? Isn't it the best phone ever?
- 그 영화에 나오는 배우들 역대급이더라. 유명한 배우들이 엄청 많아.
  The actors that appear in that movie are the best of all time. There are a ton of famous actors in it.
- 오늘 시험 진짜 역대급으로 어려웠어.
  Today's exam was seriously the most difficult exam ever.

N 이/가 역대급이다

4

Canceling and Reasons

Vocabulary

영상 화질이 떨어지다
video quality is poor

중간 중간에 화면이 끊기다
the screen cuts out in the middle

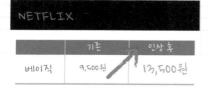

구독료가 오르다 / 인상되다
the subscription fee increases / is raised

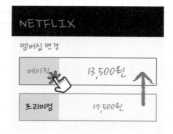

요금제를 더 싼 걸로 변경하다
to change one's subscription plan
to a cheaper one

계정을 삭제하다
to delete one's account

넷플릭스에서 디즈니플러스로
갈아타다
to change from Netflix to Disney Plus

046

1 콘텐츠가 부실하다 the content is poor

넷플릭스에 가입했는데 콘텐츠가 생각보다 부실해.
I signed up for Netflix, but the content is poorer than I thought.

2 볼 만한 게 없다 to have nothing worth watching

요즘 영화 중에 볼 만한 게 진짜 없네.
There's really nothing worth watching among the movies that are out these days.

3 왠지 잘 안 봐지다 to end up not watching for some reason

나는 왠지 드라마가 잘 안 봐지더라.
I end up not watching dramas for some reason.

4 구독료가 비싸다 the subscription fee is expensive

구독료는 비싼데 콘텐츠는 별로야.
The subscription fee is expensive, but the content is not that good.

5 가격이 부담되다 the price is burdensome

가격이 좀 부담되니까 넷플릭스랑 디즈니플러스 중에 하나만 보자.
The price is a bit burdensome, so between Netflix and Disney Plus, let's just watch one of them.

6 넷플릭스를 끊다 / 해지하다 to end / cancel one's Netflix subscription

넷플릭스를 해지하고 디즈니플러스로 갈아 탔어.
I canceled my Netflix subscription and changed to Disney Plus.

7 넷플릭스에 재가입하다 to re-subscribe to Netflix

넷플릭스 끊었다가 보고 싶은 시리즈가 있어서 재가입했어.
I canceled my Netflix subscription, but now there's a series I want to watch, so I re-subscribed.

Dialogue

Alex	There's seriously nothing worth watching on Netflix these days. Should we just cancel it?
Hyeonsu	No. Season 2 of "The Villains" comes out in four months. I've been looking forward to it so much.
Alex	Well then, the subscription fee is going up, so let's cancel it for now and then re-subscribe at that time.

047

Tips

★유일한 낙이다
to be one's only pleasure

Hyeonsu	Is it really that much? That would be annoying, so let's just keep it.
Alex	Is it really that annoying?
Hyeonsu	Can't we just watch it? Watching Netflix after getting off from work is my only pleasure.

일단 해지했다가 그때 봐서 재가입하자.

This sentence means that one should cancel a subscription first and then sign up for it again later. It implies taking action first without considering the future, and then deciding whether to take further action based on the situation later. Before and after V았/었다가, words should be used indicating actions that are opposite to each other.

● **일단 옷을 둘 다 주문했다가 하나는 환불하려고.**
I ordered both items of clothing for now, and I'm going to return one of them later.

● **일단 예약했다가 안 되면 그때 가서 취소하면 어때?** How about we make the reservation for now, and if it doesn't work out, cancel it then?

● **A: 음식을 10인분이나 준비하자고?** You want to prepare 10 servings of food?
B: 응, 일단 만들었다가 다 못 먹으면 내일 먹으면 되지.
Yeah, we can make it for now, and if we don't eat all of it, we can eat the rest tomorrow.

일단 [V] 았/었다가 ▭

그거 얼마나 한다고?

그거 얼마나 한다고? is an expression that opposes the other person's statement that something is expensive. It means that there is no need to worry because the cost is not expensive. It is in the form of a question, but the meaning is that of a statement, so there is no need to answer. It can convey a sense of dismissal, so attention should be paid to intonation.

● **A: 이게 마음에 들긴 하는데 무료 배송이 아니라 고민되네.**
I do like this, but the shipping isn't free, so I'm torn.

B: 택배비, 그거 얼마나 한다고? 마음에 들면 그냥 사.
Does the shipping really cost that much? If you like it, just buy it.

048

● **A: 이거 아까 마신 커피값이야.** This is for the coffee I drank earlier.

B: 에이, 뭐야? 그거 얼마나 한다고? 그냥 내가 살게.
Are you kidding me? It wasn't that much. I'll just pay for it.

귀찮긴 뭐가 귀찮아?

This is an expression of rebuttal that is used sarcastically when strongly denying or disagreeing with what the other person said. You must take the word from the other person's speech that you disagree with and use it in this expression. It can make the other person feel disregarded, so it must be used with caution.

● **A: 여기 가격이 좀 비싼데, 다른 식당 갈까?**
The prices here are a bit expensive. Shall we go to a different restaurant?

B: 비싸긴 뭐가 비싸? 그냥 여기서 먹자.
Is it really that expensive? Let's just eat here.

● **A: 추워서 나가기 싫어. 집에 있자.**
I don't want to go outside because it's cold. Let's just stay at home.

B: 춥긴 뭐가 추워? 두껍게 입고 나가자.
It's too cold? Just put on some warm clothes and let's go out.

● **A: 아 졸려, 더 자고 싶다.** Agh, I'm sleepy. I want to sleep more.

B: 졸리긴 뭐가 졸려? 너 열두 시간 넘게 잤잖아.
Sleepy? You slept for more than twelve hours.

A/V 긴 뭐가 A/V ?

Quick Check

Steps to Subscribing

■ to join Netflix — 넷플릭스에[1] 가 입 하 다

■ to try 1 month for free — 한 달 무료 체험을 하다

■ to share an account with one's family — 가족과 계정을 공유하다

Steps to Choosing Content

■ to choose what to watch — 뭐 볼지 고르다

■ a new series is released on Netflix — 넷플릭스에 새 시리즈가 나오다

■ season 2 will be released in March — 시즌 2가 3월에[2] ☐ ☐ ☐

■ the conclusion has not been released yet — 아직 결말이[3] ☐ ☐ ☐

■ the final episode comes out — 최종화가 올라오다

■ Min Si-ah appears in the drama — 드라마에 민시아가[4] ☐ ☐ ☐ / 출연하다

■ Min Si-ah plays the main character — 민시아가 주인공을 맡다

■ this variety show has a good response — 이 예능이 반응이 좋다

1 가입하다 2 공개되다 3 안 나다 4 나오다

■ to watch from start to finish   ¹◻◻◻하다

■ to watch all at once   한번에 ²◻◻◻ 보다

Steps to Watching

■ to watch a drama   드라마를 보다 / ³◻◻◻◻

■ to play the next episode   다음 화를 재생하다

■ to press the play button   ⁴◻◻ ◻◻을 누르다

■ to set the audio to the original language   음성을 원어로 설정하다

■ to set the subtitles to Korean   자막을 한국어로 설정하다

■ to watch a Korean movie with English dubbing   한국 영화를 영어 더빙으로 보다

■ to turn on / watch with the subtitles   자막을 켜고 보다

■ to adjust the brightness   밝기를 조절하다

■ to turn up the volume   소리를 ⁵◻◻◻

■ to turn down the volume   소리를 줄이다

■ to pause for a moment   잠깐 멈추다

■ to continue watching after momentarily pausing   잠깐 멈췄다가 ⁶◻◻◻ 보다

1 정주행   2 몰아서   3 시청하다   4 재생 버튼   5 키우다   6 이어서

■	to press the pause button	정지 버튼을 누르다
■	to watch a movie at 2x speed	영화를 2배 속으로 보다
■	to rewind	[1]⬜⬜ ⬜⬜⬜ 보다
■	to skip the boring part	지루한 부분을 건너뛰면서 보다
■	to not move a muscle and only watch Netflix	[2]⬜⬜⬜ ⬜ ⬜⬜ 넷플릭스만 보다

Reviews

■	the main actor is good at acting	주연이 [3]⬜⬜⬜ ⬜⬜⬜
■	the supporting actor has good diction	조연이 딕션이 좋다
■	the director's directing ability is good	감독의 연출이 좋다
■	the visual beauty is outstanding	영상미가 뛰어나다
■	the screenplay is solid	시나리오가 [4]⬜⬜⬜⬜
■	the plot twist is shocking	반전이 충격적이다
■	to have a plot twist at the end	결말에 [5]⬜⬜⬜ ⬜⬜
■	the story is weak	스토리가 허술하다
■	the story is dragged out	스토리를 [6]⬜⬜ ⬜⬜
■	the story is cliché	스토리가 진부하다

1 앞으로 돌려서 2 꼼짝도 안 하고 3 연기를 잘하다 4 탄탄하다 5 반전이 있다 6 질질 끌다

- the ending is absurd
  결말이 ¹ ▨ ▨ ▨ ▨
- this movie has a mix of positive and negative reviews
  이 영화는 호불호가 엇갈리다
- to be a waste of time
  시간이 ² ▨ ▨ ▨
- to get goosebumps because it's a true story
  실화라서 소름 돋다
- to be based on a novel
  소설을 원작으로 하다

Steps to Unsubscribe

- video quality is poor
  영상 화질이 ³ ▨ ▨ ▨ ▨
- the screen cuts out in the middle
  중간중간에 화면이 ⁴ ▨ ▨ ▨
- the content is poor
  콘텐츠가 부실하다
- to have nothing worth watching
  볼 만한 게 없다
- to end up not watching for some reason
  왠지 잘 안 봐지다
- the subscription fee increases / is raised
  구독료가 오르다 / 인상되다
- the subscription fee is expensive
  구독료가 비싸다
- the price is burdensome
  가격이 ⁵ ▨ ▨ ▨ ▨
- to change one's subscription plan to a cheaper one
  요금제를 더 싼 걸로 변경하다

1 어이없다 2 아깝다 3 떨어지다 4 끊기다 5 부담되다

- to end / cancel one's Netflix subscription

  넷플릭스를 [1]⬜⬜ / 해지하다

- to re-subscribe to Netflix

  넷플릭스에 재가입하다

- to change from Netflix to Disney Plus

  넷플릭스에서 디즈니플러스로 [2]⬜⬜⬜⬜

- to delete one's account

  계정을 삭제하다

1 끊다 2 갈아타다

5

저녁에 뭐 시켜 먹지?

What Should We Order for Dinner?

Using the Delivery App

Vocabulary

리뷰 Review

{ 리뷰가 좋다
the reviews are good

{ 리뷰가 별로다
the reviews are not good

별점 / 평점 Stars / Rating

{ 별점 / 평점이 높다
to have a high rating

{ 별점 / 평점이 낮다
to have a low rating

배달비 Delivery Fee

{ 배달비가 무료다
the delivery is free

{ 배달비가 비싸다
the delivery fee is expensive

{ 배달비가 많이 나오다
there is a high delivery fee

배달 시간 Delivery Time

{ 배달 시간이 오래 걸리다
the delivery takes a long time

{ 배달이 금방 오다
the delivery comes right away

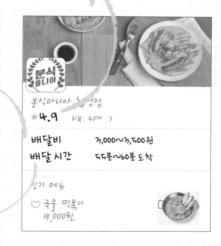

049

① 배달을 시키다 to order delivery

배달을 시키려고 하다가 배달비가 비싸서 그냥 라면 끓여 먹었어.
I was going to order delivery, but the delivery fee was expensive, so I just ate some Ramyeon.

② 음식을 배달시켜 먹다 to order delivery food and eat it

음식을 배달시켜 먹으면 편하긴 한데 쓰레기가 너무 많이 나와.
Ordering delivery food and eating is convenient, but it creates a lot of trash.

③ 오이에 알러지가 있다 to have a cucumber allergy

오이에 알러지가 있어서 오이를 먹으면 안 돼.
I have a cucumber allergy, so I can't eat cucumbers.

④ 김밥에서 오이를 빼다 to remove the cucumbers from Gimbap

김밥에서 오이 빼 주세요.
Please remove the cucumbers from the Gimbap.

⑤ 덜 맵게 하다 to make something less spicy

매운 걸 잘 못 먹어요. 덜 맵게 해 주세요.
I can't eat spicy food very well. Please make it less spicy.

Dialogue

Hyeonsu	It's bothersome to cook. Shall we order delivery food?
Alex	Sure, let's do that.
Alex	I'm craving spicy food today.
Hyeonsu	Then how about Tteokbokki?

Hyeonsu	This restaurant has good reviews. Let's order from here.
Alex	Hold on, the delivery fee is really expensive.
Hyeonsu	Hmm, then how about this place? Delivery is free, and the ratings are high.
Alex	How long does it say it will take?
Hyeonsu	It won't take long. About 20 minutes?
Alex	Okay, cool.

밥 하기 귀찮은데 배달시켜 먹을까?

This expression is used when suggesting to order delivery food. A/V은/는데 can be used to explain the reason and the situation.

● **지금 바빠서 정신이 없는데 배달시켜 먹을까?**
I'm scatterbrained because I'm so busy. Shall we order delivery?

● **오늘 입맛이 없는데 배달시켜 먹을까?**
I don't have an appetite today. Shall we order delivery?

● **뭔가 맛있는 거 먹고 싶은데 배달시켜 먹을까?**
I want to eat something tasty. Shall we order delivery?

A/V 은/는데 배달시켜 먹을까?

NS
매운 음식이 좀 땡겨.

땡기다 is a non-standard word, and the appropriate form is 당기다. 당기다 means that one has a sudden craving or appetite for something. It can be used when one wants to eat a specific food. The appropriate form is 매운 음식이 당겨, but 매운 음식이 땡겨 is far more commonly used.

● **갑자기 피자가 땡기네. 오늘 점심은 피자다!**
I'm suddenly craving pizza. Today's lunch will be pizza!

● **날씨가 쌀쌀해서 국물 있는 음식이 땡긴다.**
The weather is chilly, so I want to eat something with broth.

● **오늘은 외식이 안 땡겨. 그냥 집에서 먹자.**
I don't feel like eating outside today. Let's just eat at home.

N 이/가 땡기다

051

얼마 안 걸려.

When 얼마 is used with a negation 안, it emphasizes that the quantity, value, or degree of something is small without revealing a specific number. 얼마 안 걸리다 indicates a short amount of time, while 얼마 안 하 다 indicates a small amount of money. 얼마 안 되다 is used in variety of situation to indicate a small amount of time, money, distance, etc.

- **나도 도착한 지 얼마 안 됐어.**
  It hasn't been that long since I arrived, either.

- **이 김밥 얼마 안 해. 그냥 내가 살게.**
  This Gimbap doesn't cost much. I'll just pay for it.

- **이 요리는 시간이 얼마 안 걸리는 간단한 요리야.**
  This is a simple dish that doesn't take long to cook.

얼마 안

2

Confirming and Serving Delivery Food

Vocabulary

음식이 새서 오다
the food arrives leaking

음식을 데워서 먹다
to heat up food and eat it

음식이 오다 / 도착하다
the food arrives / comes

음식을 렌지에 돌려서 먹다
to microwave food and eat it

테이블에 수저를 놓다
to set spoons and chopsticks on the table

음식을 덜어서 먹다
to take a portion of food

음식을 미리 좀 덜어 놓다
to divide food into portions in advance

052

① **음식이 늦게 오다** the food arrives late

A: 음식이 너무 늦게 왔어. The food arrived so late.
B: 응, 얼른 먹자. 점심 시간 10분 밖에 안 남았어.
Yeah, let's hurry and eat. We only have 10 minutes of lunch time left.

② **배달 사고가 나다** a delivery accident occurs

포장 뚜껑이 열려서 국물이 다 새는 배달 사고가 났어요.
A delivery accident occurred that caused the package lid to open and all the soup leaked out.

③ **음식이 잘못 오다** the wrong food arrives

음식이 잘못 왔어요. 물냉면을 시켰는데 비빔냉면이 왔어요.
The wrong food arrived. I ordered Mul-naengmyeon, but I received Bibim-naengmyeon.

④ **1인분 덜 오다** to receive 1 portion less

3인분을 주문했는데 1인분이 덜 왔어요. I ordered 3 servings, but received 1 portion less.

⑤ **반찬이 안 오다** to not receive any side dishes

반찬이 안 와서 식당에 전화했어. I didn't get any side dishes, so I called the restaurant.

⑥ **밥을 빠뜨리고 오다** to arrive without any rice

비빔밥을 시켰는데 밥을 빠뜨리고 왔더라.
I ordered Bibimbap, but it arrived without any rice.

⑦ **음식이 식어서 오다** the food arrives cold

음식이 식어서 와서 렌지에 돌려서 먹으려고 해.
The food arrived cold, so I'm going to heat it up in the microwave.

⑧ **면이 불어서 오다** the noodles arrive soggy

면이 불어서 와서 도저히 먹을 수 없어요.
The noodles arrived soggy, so I just can't eat them.

Dialogue

Alex The food is here! Wow, the portions from this place are totally awesome.

Hyeonsu I don't think we can eat all of it. Shall we divide the food into portions in advance?

Alex Yeah, let's just take out as much as we can eat.

Hyeonsu	But the food arrived kind of cold, probably because the delivery took a long time to get here.
Alex	You're right. Well then, we can just warm it up before we eat it.
Hyeonsu	Yeah, I'll put it in the microwave. You set the spoons and chopsticks on the table.

먹을 만큼만 덜어서 먹자.

먹을 만큼만 is an expression that indicates only the amount that one will/can eat—neither too much nor too little. As such, 먹을 만큼만 덜어서 먹자 is suggesting to take only the appropriate portion to eat.

- 안 남기게 먹을 만큼만 가지고 가.
  Only take as much as you can eat, so you don't have any left over.

- 먹을 만큼만 시키자. 남으면 어떡해?
  Let's only order as much as we can eat. What would we do with the leftovers?

- 너무 많이 만들지 말고 먹을 만큼만 만들면 돼.
  Let's not make too much and only make as much as we can eat.

먹을 만큼만 ▮▮▮▮▮▮

덜어서 먹자.

덜어서 먹다 means to take a certain amount and eat that portion. V아/어서 is used to connect actions that are in continuity with each other.

- **데워(서) 먹다** 음식이 식었는데 데워서 먹자.
  The food is cold. Let's heat it up and then eat it.

- **끓여(서) 먹다** 배가 좀 고파서 라면 하나 끓여 먹었어.
  I was a bit hungry, so I made some instant noodles and ate them.

- **볶아(서) 먹다** 채소를 볶아서 먹으면 맛도 좋고 건강에도 좋다. If you stir-fry vegetables and then eat them, they taste good and it's also good for your health.

- **나눠(서) 먹다** 주문한 음식을 같이 나눠 먹자.
  Let's share the food we ordered and eat together.

V 아/어서 먹다

오래 걸려서 그런지 음식이 좀 식어서 왔어.

오래 걸려서 그런지 was used when guessing that the reason why the food was cold when it arrived was probably because the delivery took a long time, but it's not certain. A/V아/어서 그런지 is an expression that guesses a reason. It can be used when it seems that it may be the reason or the cause of a later result, but it cannot be determined with complete certainty.

- 배달료가 비싸서 그런지 배달 주문이 줄었어. The amount of delivery orders has decreased, probably because the delivery fee is expensive.
- 날씨가 더워져서 그런지 아이스커피가 잘 팔려.
  Iced-coffee is selling well, maybe because the weather has gotten warmer.
- 잠을 많이 못 자서 그런지 몸이 좀 안 좋아.
  Maybe it's because I didn't sleep much, I don't feel very well.

A/V 아/어서 그런지

먹으면 되지, 뭐.

A/V으면 되다 can be used when presenting a simple solution. However, if one does not feel completely happy with the solution, but it doesn't cause much of an issue, the expression A/V으면 되지, 뭐 is used.

- 젓가락이 없으면 포크로 먹으면 되지, 뭐.
  If there aren't any chopsticks, I guess I can just eat with a fork.
- 좀 기다렸다가 먹으면 되지, 뭐. Well, we can just wait a bit before we eat.
- 나중에 하면 되지, 뭐. 급한 거 없어. We can just do it later. There's nothing urgent.

A/V 으면 되지, 뭐.

3

Eating Food

밥을 국물에 말아서 먹다
to put rice in one's soup and eat it

남은 음식을 냉장고에 넣다
to put leftover food in the fridge

같이 나눠서 먹다
to share and eat together

밥을 양념에 비벼서 먹다
to mix rice with seasoning and eat it

쌈을 싸서 먹다
to make a lettuce wrap and eat it

쌈장에 찍어서 먹다
to dip something into Ssamjang and eat it

055

① 음식 양이 많다 / 푸짐하다 the amount of food is large / plentiful

2인분을 시켰는데 양이 푸짐해서 세 명이 먹을 수 있었어요.
We ordered 2 servings, but the portions were so large that three of us could eat it.

② 양이 부족하다 the amount is not enough

양이 부족하면 이따가 다른 거 더 먹으면 돼.
If the amount isn't enough, you can eat something else later.

③ 한입 먹다 to eat a bite

이거 진짜 맛있어. 한입 먹어 봐.
This is really delicious. Try a bite.

④ 밥을 볶아서 먹다 to fry rice and eat it

간단하게 김치랑 밥을 볶아서 먹자.
Let's simply fry some rice and Kimchi and eat it.

⑤ 음식이 남다 to have leftover food

맛이 별로 없어서 그런지 음식이 많이 남았어.
Maybe it's because the food didn't taste that good, I have a lot of food leftover.

⑥ 다 먹고 치우다 to finish eating and clean up

저녁 다 먹고 치우면 아홉 시가 돼.
By the time we finish eating dinner and clean up, it's 9:00.

Dialogue

Alex	Wow, this was really delicious.
Hyeonsu	Yeah, I ate so well. I seriously feel like my stomach's going to burst.
Alex	We have to fry rice in the leftover soup. Fried rice is an absolute must.

Hyeonsu	You think you can eat more?
Alex	Even if I'm full, I can't resist eating fried rice.
Hyeonsu	I don't think I can eat any more.
Alex	Then even if you ask for just one bite later, I'm not giving you any.

배 터질 것 같아.

터지다 means that something explodes or bursts, so it is used with 풍선이 터지다(a balloon bursts), 폭탄이 터지다(a bomb explodes). 배가 터질 것 같다 is an expression used when you eat a lot of something and your stomach is so full that you can't eat any more, like a balloon popping.

- **너무 많이 먹어서 배가 터질 것 같아.**
  I ate way too much, so I feel like my stomach is going to burst.

- **배가 터질 것 같은데 디저트는 먹고 싶어.**
  I feel like my stomach is going to burst, but I want to eat dessert.

- **배 터지게 먹었더니 너무 졸려.**
  I ate until my stomach was bursting, so now I'm really sleepy.

배가 터지다

NS **BW**

국룰

국룰 is a new word that is short for 국민의 룰(national rule). The 룰 in 국룰 comes from the English word "rule." But it does not mean a mandatory rule; rather, it is a humorous expression of a common behavior that is naturally performed among many people. It is mainly used in the form N 은/는 국룰이다.

- **식사 후 커피 한 잔은 국룰이야.** A cup of coffee after a meal is an absolute must.

- **라면 먹을 때 김치는 국룰이야.** One must eat Ramyeon with Kimchi.

- **축구 볼 때 치킨과 맥주는 국룰.**
  It's a national rule that one must have chicken and beer while watching soccer.

N 은/는 국룰이다

057

BW

볶음밥은 못 참지.

참다 means "to endure," and is used in phrases such as 눈물을 참다(to hold back tears), 화를 참다(to hold back one's anger). However, N은/는 못 참지 is an expression that caught on and became a fad phrase. It means that something is too good to be resisted and absolutely must be done.

- **이건 못 참지.** I can't resist this.

- **귀여운 건 못 참지. 이건 꼭 사야 돼.** I can't resist cute things. I have to buy this.

- **50%나 할인한다고? 세일은 못 참지.** It's 50% off? I can't resist a sale.

N 은/는 못 참지.

나중에 한입만 달라고 해도 안 준다.

한입 indicates an amount of food that can be eating in just one bite. And it is usually said as 한입만 (줘), 한입만 먹을게 when you ask your close friend or family member for a bite of their food because it looks delicious. Sometimes, when making or ordering food, some people say that they won't eat it, but when they see the food, they change their minds and ask to share it. In that case, you can say 나중에 한입만 달라고 해도 안 줄 거야 while preparing food, which means that you will absolutely not share it with them when the food comes out.

- **라면 맛있어? 나도 한입만!** Is Ramyeon tasty? Let me try just one bite!

- **맛있어 보인다. 한입만 먹을게.** That looks good. I'll just have a taste.

- **딱 1인분만 시켰으니까 나중에 한입만 달라고 해도 안 줄 거야.**
  I only ordered exactly 1 portion, so even if you ask for a taste later, I won't give it to you.

4

Leaving Reviews

Vocabulary

리뷰를 쓰다 / 남기다
to write / leave a review

별점 만점을 주다
to give a perfect score

포장이 깔끔하다
the packaging is neat

포장 상태가 엉망이다
the packaging is a mess

음식이 전체적으로 만족스럽다
to be overall satisfied with the food

맛이 변해서 아쉽다
to be a shame that the taste changed

058

① **별점을 주다** to give (a number of) stars

별점을 몇 개 주면 좋을까?
How many stars should I give them?

② **별을 한 개 빼다** to take off one star

다 좋은데 배달이 너무 늦어서 별을 한 개 뺐어요.
Everything was good, but the delivery arrived really late, so I took off one star.

③ **매일 먹어도 안 질리다** to not get sick of something even if one eats it every day

너무 맛있어서 1주일에 세 번은 시켜 먹는데 매일 먹어도 안 질릴 거 같아요.
It's so delicious that I order it 3 times a week, but I don't think I'd get sick of it even if I eat it every day.

④ **간이 좀 약하다** the seasoning is a bit weak

난 싱겁게 먹는 편이라 간이 좀 약한 게 좋아.
I usually eat food that's on the bland side, so I like the seasoning to be a bit weak.

⑤ **간이 너무 세다** the seasoning is too strong

간이 너무 세서 많이 먹기 힘들어.
The seasoning is too strong, so it's difficult to eat a lot.

⑥ **맛이 자극적이다** the flavor is pungent

맛이 자극적이라 맛있긴 한데 나중에 배탈 날 것 같아.
It's delicious because the flavor is pungent, but I think I'll have an upset stomach later.

⑦ **음식에서 머리카락이 나오다** a hair appears in the food

음식에서 머리카락이 나왔어요. 환불해 주세요.
There was a hair in my food. Please give me a refund.

⑧ **앞으로도 자주 애용하다** to patronize often in the future as well

맛도 서비스도 좋았어요. 앞으로도 자주 애용할게요.
The taste and service were both good. I'll buy from here often in the future as well.

Dialogue

리뷰

먹방대왕 〉
★★★★

음식이 살짝 새서 오긴 했지만 음식 맛은 최고였
어요. 포장에 신경 좀 더 써 주세요.

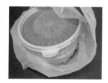

잘먹고잘살자 〉
★★★★★

평점이 높은 데는 이유가 다 있네요.
찐맛집이에요.

Tips

★**살짝** a bit, slightly

 Although the food was leaking a bit when it arrived, the taste was the best. Please pay more attention to the packaging.

 There's a reason why the ratings are so high. This is truly a good restaurant.

059

← **리뷰**

 냥냥 7
★★★★★

자극적이지 않게 맛있어서 하나도 남김없이
다 먹었어요. 게다가 가격에 비해 양도 많아
가성비도 훌륭합니다. 나중에도 자꾸 생각날
것 같아요. 앞으로 단골 예약이에요.

Tips
★**남김없이** without leaving any leftovers
★**자꾸** continuously, repeatedly
★**단골** regular (customer)

 It was delicious without being too strong, so I ate it all without leaving any leftovers. In addition, the portion is large compared to the price, so it's an excellent value for the money. I think I'll keep thinking of it even later. I'll be a regular (customer) here from now on.

평점이 높은 데는 이유가 다 있네요.

이유가 다 있다 means that there must be a reason for a certain incident or result. In particular, when anyone could accept the results, the expression A/V은/는 데는 이유가 다 있다 is used, and the result should be written in front of A/V은/는 데. 평점이 높은 데는 이유가 다 있네요 means that one can understand why the ratings are high.

- 인기가 많은 데는 이유가 다 있네요. There's a reason why it's so popular.

- 줄을 서서 기다리는 데는 이유가 다 있었어요.
  There was a reason why people were waiting in line.

- 걔가 성적이 좋은 데는 이유가 다 있어. No wonder why she gets good grades.

A/V 은/는 데는 이유가 다 있다

NS BW

찐맛집

찐 is an emphasized pronunciation of the 진 in 진짜. It has become a prefix meaning "the best," "really good," or "not a lie." 찐맛집 is a new word combining 찐 and 맛집, indicating restaurant that genuinely offers delicious food, rather than one that became famous through social media promotions. The word 찐 is also used in phrases such as N이/가 찐이다 or 찐으로.

> **Tips**
> ★찐친
> 찐친 is short for 찐친구(true friend).

- 찐사랑, 찐팬, *찐친
  true love, true fan, true friend

- 이 집 고기는 찐이다. 올해 먹은 고기 중 최고야.
  The meat at this restaurant is the real deal. It's the best out of all the meat I've eaten this year.

060

● **오늘은 찐으로 재밌었다.** Today was truly fun.

N 이/가 찐이다

NS BW

가성비

가성비 is short for 가격 대비 성능의 비율(price to performance ratio). It is a new word that refers to the degree of performance, quality, or efficiency in comparison with a set price. It is usually used in the phrases 가성비가 좋다(to be a good value for the money), 가성비가 훌륭하다(to be an excellent value for the money), 가성비 맛집(a place that is a good value), 가성비가 별로다(to not have a very good value for the money).

● **가성비 좋은 노트북 좀 추천해 줘.**
Please recommend a laptop that is a good value compared to the price.

● **이 가격에 디저트까지 포함이라니 가성비가 아주 좋다.**
They even include dessert in the price, so it's a really good value.

● **이 호텔은 가격에 비해 시설이나 서비스가 너무 좋아. 가성비가 훌륭해.**
The facilities and service at this hotel are great for the price. It's an excellent value.

Quick Check

Ordering Delivery

- to order delivery

  배달을[1] 시 키 다

- to order delivery food and eat it

  음식을 배달시켜 먹다

- to recommend a dish

  메뉴를 추천하다

Finding a Good Restaurant Through an App

- to have a high rating

  [2] ▨▨ / ▨▨ 이 높다

- to have a low rating

  별점 / 평점이 낮다

- the reviews are good

  리뷰가 좋다

- the reviews are not good

  리뷰가[3] ▨▨▨

- the delivery fee is expensive

  배달비가 비싸다 /

  [4] ▨▨ ▨▨▨

- the delivery is free

  배달비가 무료다

- the delivery takes a long time

  배달 시간이 오래 걸리다

- the delivery comes right away

  배달이 금방 오다

Making a Request While Ordering

to have a cucumber allergy	오이에 알러지가 있다
to remove the cucumbers from Gimbap	김밥에서 오이를 ¹⬛⬛
to make something less spicy	²⬛ ⬛⬛ 하다

Delivery Confirmation and Issues

the food arrives / comes	음식이 오다 / 도착하다
the food arrives late	음식이 늦게 오다
a delivery accident occurs	³⬛⬛ ⬛⬛ 가 나다
the wrong food arrives	음식이 잘못 오다
to receive 1 portion less	1인분 ⁴⬛⬛
to not receive any side dishes	반찬이 안 오다
to arrive without any rice	⁵⬛⬛ ⬛⬛⬛⬛ 오다
the food arrives leaking	음식이 새서 오다
the food arrives cold	⁶⬛⬛ ⬛⬛⬛ 오다
the noodles arrive soggy	면이 불어서 오다

---

1 빼다 2 덜 맵게 3 배달 사고 4 덜 오다 5 밥을 빠뜨리고 6 음식이 식어서

Eating Food

- to heat up food and eat it

  ¹ ⬜⬜⬜ ⬜⬜⬜ 먹다

- to take a portion of food

  음식을 덜어서 먹다

- to divide food into portions in advance

  음식을 미리 좀 덜어 놓다

- to microwave food and eat it

  음식을 ² ⬜⬜⬜ ⬜⬜⬜ 먹다

- to set spoons and chopsticks on the table

  테이블에 수저를 놓다

- to eat a bite

  한입 먹다

- to share and eat together

  ³ ⬜⬜ ⬜⬜⬜ 먹다

- to put rice in one's soup and eat it

  밥을 국물에 말아서 먹다

- to fry rice and eat it

  밥을 볶아서 먹다

- to mix rice with seasoning and eat it

  밥을 양념에 비벼서 먹다

- to make a lettuce wrap and eat it

  쌈을 싸서 먹다

- to dip something into Ssamjang and eat it

  쌈장에 찍어서 먹다

- to have leftover food

  음식이 ⁴ ⬜⬜

- to put leftover food in the fridge

  남은 음식을 냉장고에 넣다

---

1 음식을 데워서 2 렌지에 돌려서 3 같이 나눠서 4 남다

■ to finish eating and clean up	다 먹고 [1] ⬜⬜⬜	

Reviews and Ratings

■ to write / leave a review	리뷰를 쓰다 / [2] ⬜⬜⬜
■ to give (a number of) stars	별점을 주다
■ to give a perfect score	별점 [3] ⬜⬜ 을 주다
■ to take off one star	별을 한 개 빼다
■ the packaging is neat	포장이 깔끔하다
■ the packaging is a mess	포장 상태가 [4] ⬜⬜⬜⬜
■ to not get sick of something even if one eats it every day	매일 먹어도 [5] ⬜⬜⬜
■ the amount of food is large / plentiful	음식 양이 많다 / [6] ⬜⬜⬜⬜
■ the amount is not enough	양이 부족하다
■ the seasoning is a bit weak	간이 좀 약하다
■ the seasoning is too strong	간이 너무 세다
■ the flavor is pungent	맛이 자극적이다
■ a hair appears in the food	음식에서 머리카락이 [7] ⬜⬜⬜
■ to be overall satisfied with the food	음식이 전체적으로 만족스럽다

1 치우다 2 남기다 3 만점 4 엉망이다 5 안 질리다 6 푸짐하다 7 나오다

- to be a shame that the taste changed　맛이 변해서 ¹▨▨▨

- to patronize often in the future as well　앞으로도 자주 애용하다

1 아쉽다

6

우리 만날래?

Want to Meet Up?

Deciding on a Place via KakaoTalk

Vocabulary

카카오톡 KakaoTalk

문자 메시지 text message

단톡방 Group Chat
- **단톡방을 만들다**
  to make a group chat
- **단톡방에 친구를 초대하다**
  to invite a friend to
  a group chat

투표 Polls
- **단톡방에 투표를 올리다**
  to make a poll in
  a group chat
- **투표를 하다**
  to vote
- **금요일이 많이 나오다**
  Friday gets the most
  votes

링크 Links
- **링크를 남기다**
  to leave a link
- **링크를 보내다**
  to send a link
- **링크를 공유하다**
  to share a link
- **링크를 확인하다**
  to check a link

Tips

★ 카카오톡 KakaoTalk

카카오톡(KakaoTalk), 카톡(KaTalk) or 톡(Talk) for short, is Korea's most widely known messenger app. KaTalk is widely used not only for public functions but for private social gatherings as well. Friends who hang out frequently or family members have group chats called 단톡방 that they use to share photos and information. In particular, when arranging a gathering, you can use the poll function to determine the meeting time and location, and any costs at the gathering can easily be divided and paid equally using settlement function.

① 카톡을 하다 to use KaTalk

A: 오늘 너무 재미있었어. 조심해서 가.
Today was super fun. Get home safely.

B: 응, 잘 가. 나중에 카톡할게.
Yeah, see you. I'll KaTalk you later.

② 톡을 보내다 to send a KaTalk message

A: 니가 아까 보낸 톡을 아직 못 봤어.
I haven't looked at the KaTalk message you sent.

B: 톡으로 자료 보냈으니까 꼭 확인해 봐.
I sent you some materials via KaTalk, so make sure you check it.

③ 톡이 안 오다 the KaTalk message does not arrive

A: 마엘한테 아직 톡 안 왔어?
Hasn't the KaTalk message come from Mael yet?

B: 어! 지금 왔다. 갑자기 일이 생겨서 좀 늦을 거라는데.
Oh! It just came. Mael said she got caught up in something suddenly, so it might be a bit late.

④ 단톡방에서 나가다 to leave a group chat

A: 현수가 단톡방에서 안 보이던데?
I don't see Hyeonsu in the group chat.

B: 응, 며칠 전에 단톡방에서 나갔어. 알렉스하고 싸웠대.
Yeah, he left the gruop chat a few days ago. I heard that he had a fight with Alex.

⑤ 링크를 눌러서 들어가다 to click and follow a link

A: 이 영상 진짜 웃겨. 링크 눌러서 들어가 봐.
This video is so funny. Click and follow this link.

B: 아, 강아지 너무 귀엽다.
Oh, the puppy is so cute.

Dialogue

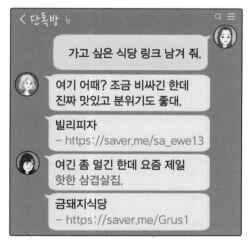

Mael   Let's all go and eat something yummy together next Friday.

Yuna   Yeah. I'll make a group chat and invite our friends.

Yuna   Leave some links to any restaurants you want to go to.

Mael   How about this place? It's a bit pricey, but I heard it's super good, and the vibe is great too.

Ing   This place is a bit far, but it's the hottest Samgyeopsal restaurant these days.

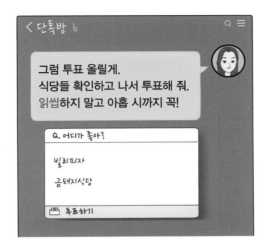

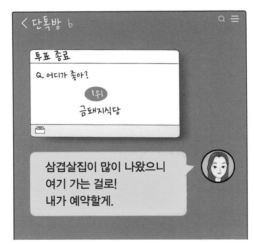

Yuna   Then I'll make a poll. Check out the restaurants and vote. Don't leave me on read and make sure to vote by 9:00!

Yuna   The Samgyeopsal place got the most votes, so we'll go here! I'll make the reservation.

ㅇㅇ

When writing a simple answer in a messenger app, if the recipient can sufficiently guess the meaning, you can just write the initial consonants instead of writing out the whole word. "ㄱㅅ" instead of 감사합니다, "ㅅㄱ" instead of 수고하세요, "ㅇㅋ" instead of 오케이, and "ㅇㅇ" instead of 응 are used to increase efficiency.

핫한 삼겹살 집

This means that the Samgyeopsal restaurant is very popular. 핫하다 combines the English word "hot" with 하다, and is used for things that have recently become very popular. 핫플레이스(hot place), which means a popular place, is often shortened to 핫플.

- 그 카페 완전 핫해. 생긴 지 얼마 안 됐는데 인기가 많아.
  That café is a super hot place. It hasn't been that long since it's opened, but it's really popular.

- 요즘 제일 핫한 여행지라 숙소 예약하기 힘들대.
  It's the most popular travel destination these days, so it's difficult to reserve accommodations.

- 홍대 핫플 추천 좀 해 줘. Please recommend a hot place in Hongdae.

N 이/가 핫하다

NS **BW** **IL**

읽씹

It is possible to check whether a recipient has read a message or not on KakaoTalk. When the recipient does not reply even though they have read the message, the expression 읽씹 is used. 읽씹 is short for 읽고 씹다, and 씹다 means "to ignore." You must be careful when using 읽씹 because 씹다 is a crude word.

● **세 시간째 읽씹. 무슨 일이 있는 거야?**
He's left me on read for three hours. What's going on?

● **내 톡을 계속 읽씹하는 이유가 뭘까?**
I wonder why she keeps leaving my Katalk messages on read?

N 을/를 읽씹하다

2

Reserving and Notifying

Vocabulary

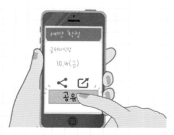

예약 확인 문자를 공유하다
to share a reservation confirmation message

금요일에는 만석이다
there are no seats available on Friday

예약 날짜를 토요일로 변경하다
to change the reservation day to Saturday

예약을 취소하다
to cancel a reservation

지도 링크를 걸다
to link a map

지도를 보고 잘 찾아오다
to find one's way by looking at a map

064

① 박유나 이름으로 식당을 예약하다
to make a reservation at a restaurant under the name Park Yuna

박유나 이름으로 식당을 예약했습니다. 늦지 않게 와 주시기 바랍니다.
I have made a restaurant reservation under the name Park Yuna. Please arrive on time.

② 창가 / 테라스 / 개별 룸으로 예약하다
to reserve a window seat / terrace / private room

조용히 얘기 나누고 싶어서 개별 룸으로 예약했어.
I want to be able to talk quietly with you, so I reserved a private room.

③ 예약이 확정되다
a reservation is confirmed

예약이 확정됐다고 카톡이 왔어.
I got a KaTalk message that the reservation has been confirmed.

④ 예약이 다 차다
reservations are fully booked

벌써 예약이 다 찼대. 다른 곳으로 알아보자.
They said that their reservations are already fully booked. Let's look for a different place.

⑤ 대기자 명단 / 대기 리스트에 이름을 올리다
to put one's name on a waiting list

만석이긴 한데 대기 리스트에 이름을 올려 달라고 했어.
They're full, but they told us to put our name on the waiting list.

Dialogue

Tips
★완료 completion

Yuna Reservation made under the name Park Yuna for 7:00 on Friday at the Golden Pig Restaurant!

Yuna It seems like a seriously popular place.

It's really tough to get a reservation here.

065

Tips

★**겨우** barely, only just
★**필수** required, necessary

Yuna I couldn't make a reservation at their 1st branch because they were full, but I just barely managed to make one at the 2nd branch nearby.

Yuna Don't get confused and make sure to come to the right one.

Yuna I left a map link, so make sure to check it!!

NS

맞는 듯.

맞는 듯 is a shortened form of 맞는 듯하다, meaning "seems right" or "seems to be correct." A/V은/는/을 듯하다 is not commonly used in everyday conversation. However, its shortened form A/V은/는/을 듯 is frequently used in messaging apps for efficiency.

● **오늘 좀 늦을 듯.** It seems like I'll be a bit late today.

● **커피를 안 좋아하는 듯.** She doesn't seem to like coffee.

● **엄마 기분이 좀 안 좋은 듯. 조심하자.**
Mom seems to be in a bad mood. Let's be careful.

A/V 은/는/을 듯.

NS **BW** **IL**

빡세.

빡세다 is a dialect that means something is very difficult and tough to do. These days, it is used all over the country, but it has a crude tone, so you need to be careful when using it.

● **이번 강의는 과제도 많고 발표도 있어서 너무 빡세.**
This lecture is super intense because there are a lot of assignments and presentations.

● **월요일부터 너무 빡세다.** Things have been way too busy since Monday.

● **빡세게 운동했더니 다리가 아프다.** I worked out too hard, so my legs hurt.

N 이/가 빡세다

066

헷갈리지 말고 잘 찾아와.

When making a command or request, adding the negative form V지 말고 in front of it further emphasizes the command or request.

- 그거 다 먹지 말고 남겨 둬. Don't eat all of that and leave some leftover.

- 급하게 오지 말고 천천히 와. Don't rush over here and come slowly.

- 많이 사지 말고 필요한 것만 사. Don't buy a lot and only buy what you need.

 **V** 지 말고 imperative

At a Restaurant

Vocabulary

자리가 다 차다
all the seats are full

자리가 나다
a seat is open

*벨을 누르다
to press the bell

*진동벨이 울리다
a buzzer vibrates

음식에 마늘이 들어가 있다
to have garlic in the food

남은 음식을 싸다/포장하다
to pack up leftover food

음식을 가지러 가다
to go get the food

주문한 음식이 나오다
the food that was ordered
is ready

> **Tips**
>
> **＊벨**
> In large Korean restaurants, since sound does not carry well, each table has a bell to call the server.
>
> **＊진동벨**
> At coffee shops in Korea, an employee will give you a buzzer when you place your order. When the buzzer vibrates, you can take it to the pickup area and receive your order.

067

① **자리를 안내할 때까지 잠깐 기다리다**
to wait a moment before being shown to one's seat / table

자리 안내해 드릴 때까지 여기에서 잠깐 기다려 주세요.
Please wait here a moment until you are shown to your table.

② **편한 자리에 앉다** to sit wherever you'd like

편한 자리에 앉으시면 됩니다.
You may sit wherever you'd like.

③ **세 명 자리가 없다** to have no tables for three people

세 명 자리가 없어서 좀 기다려야 된대.
They said we have to wait because there are no tables for three people.

④ **메뉴를 고르다** to choose what to eat

일단 메뉴부터 고르자. 뭐 먹을까?
Let's choose what to eat first. What shall we eat?

⑤ **메뉴를 추천해 달라고 하다** to ask someone to recommend what to eat

뭘 먹을지 모르겠다. 그냥 메뉴를 추천해 달라고 하자.
I don't know what to eat. Let's just ask them to recommend something.

⑥ **음식을 시키다 / 주문하다** to order food

저기요, 음식 주문할게요.
Excuse me, we'd like to order.

⑦ **밥이 아직 안 나오다** the food hasn't come out yet

주문한 지 20분이 지났는데 밥이 아직 안 나왔어요.
It's been 20 minutes since we ordered, but the food still hasn't come out yet.

⑧ **1인분 더 추가로 주문하다** to order one additional serving

이거랑 같은 걸로 1인분 더 추가로 주문할게요.
We'll order one additional serving of the same thing.

Dialogue

Ryo   What should we order? What do you want to eat?
Alex   Their Samgyeopsal is famous, so let's eat that first.
Alex   Whoa, amazing! This is happiness right here.

068

Tips
★밑반찬 side dish

Ryo	Ooh, you're making the frown of truth. Is it really that delicious?
Ing	Ryo, you hurry and try some too. It's wicked good.
Ing	Should we ask for more side dishes?
Ryo	The side dishes are self-service here. I'll go and get some more.

BW

진실의 미간

미간 refers to the area between one's eyebrows. Generally, one furrows their eyebrows when they are emotionally agitated, so frowning or furrowing one's brow is considered an honest reaction without lying. In particular, when we eat delicious food, we often furrow our brows while admiring the taste, so that is why it's called 진실의 미간(the frown of truth). It is used in forms such as 진실의 미간이 나오다.

- **저 반응은 찐이야. 진실의 미간이 나왔잖아.**
  That reaction is real. He made the frown of truth.

- **숨길 수 없는 진실의 미간.**
  The frown of truth that can't be hidden.

When you see another person really enjoying delicious food and ask if the food is that delicious, 그렇게 맛있어? is used. This expression is used to ask with a bit of surprise whether the other person's emotions or feelings expressed through their facial expression or actions are really that strong.

- **그렇게 재미있어?** Is it really that fun?

- **그렇게 좋아?** Do you like it that much?

- **그렇게 신나?** Are you that excited?

그렇게 █████████?

069

(더) 달라고 할까?

This is an expression used when discussing with one's companion about ordering additional food at a restaurant. '(더) 주세요'라고 할까? is changed to indirect speech (더) 달라고 할까? and became commonly used expression.

- **1인분 더 달라고 할까?** Shall we order one more serving?

- **물 좀 더 달라고 할까?** Should we ask for some more water?

- **개인 접시 달라고 할까?** Shall we ask for individual plates?

N (을/를) 더 달라고 할까?

NS

셀프

셀프 서비스 is the English phrase "self-service" written in Korean alphabet, and it is also shortened to 셀프. In restaurants, you can often see a sign that says 물은 셀프입니다, which means that customers should get their own water. In addition, in Korea, side dishes are provided for free, and there is a corner for side dishes in one part of the restaurant so customers can get their own side dishes, bring them to their table, and eat them. Usually water, side dishes, and individual plates are 셀프 서비스 .

- **물과 반찬은 셀프 서비스입니다.** Water and side dishes are self-service.

N 은/는 셀프(서비스)이다

4

Paying and Settling up

Vocabulary

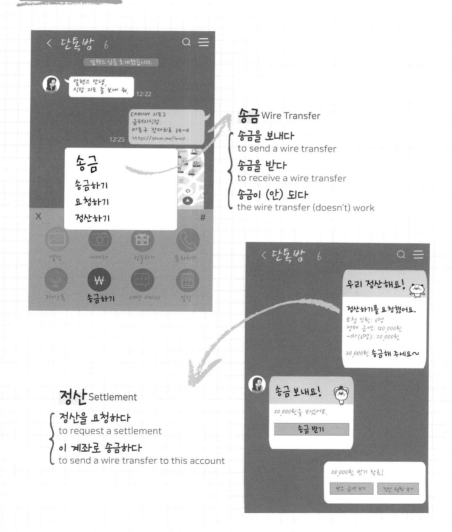

송금 Wire Transfer

송금을 보내다
to send a wire transfer

송금을 받다
to receive a wire transfer

송금이 (안) 되다
the wire transfer (doesn't) work

정산 Settlement

정산을 요청하다
to request a settlement

이 계좌로 송금하다
to send a wire transfer to this account

070

① 음식값을 카드 / 현금으로 계산하다
to pay the cost of the food with a credit card / cash

음식값은 카드로 계산할게요. I'll pay for the food with a credit card.

② 음식값을 계좌 이체하다 to send a bank transfer for the cost of the food

음식값을 계좌 이체해도 될까요? Can I pay for the food via bank transfer?

③ 핸드폰을 여기에 대다 to put one's cell phone here

A: 핸드폰으로 계산할게요. I'll pay using my phone.
B: 핸드폰을 여기에 대 주세요. Please place your phone here.

④ 카드를 여기에 꽂다 to insert one's credit card here

카드를 직접 여기에 꽂아 주세요. Please insert your card here.

⑤ 여기에 서명하다 to sign here

여기에 서명해 주세요. Please sign here.

⑥ 영수증을 버리다 to throw away the receipt

A: 영수증 드릴까요? Would you like your receipt?
B: 영수증은 버려 주세요. Please throw away the receipt.

⑦ 각자 계산하다 to pay individually

자기가 먹은 음식값은 각자 계산하자. Let's each pay individually for what we ate.

⑧ 일단 한꺼번에 계산하고 나중에 정산하다
to pay all at once first and settle up later

각자 계산하면 복잡하니까 일단 한꺼번에 계산하고 나중에 정산하자.
Paying individually would be complicated, so let's have one person pay for it all at once and settle up later.

⑨ 계좌 번호를 알려 주다 to let someone know one's bank account number

계좌 번호 알려 줄 테니까 거기로 송금해 줘.
I'll let you know my bank account number, so send a wire transfer here.

Dialogue

Ryo   How much was the Samgyeopsal?

Hyeonsu   It was about 160,000 won. I'll pay the total amount today.
Let's settle up later.

Hyeonsu   Today, the Samgyeopsal at round 1 was 160,000 won, the bar we went to for
round 2 was 100,000 won, and the Noraebang we went to for round 3 was
40,000 won, for a total of 300,000 won.

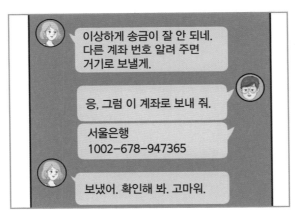

A settlement has been requested.
Number of people: 6
Total amount: 300,000 won
Round 1: 160,000 won
Round 2: 100,000 won
Round 3: 40,000 won
Please send a wire transfer for 50,000 won.

Tips

★요청 인원
requested number of people

Mael	Weird, the wire transfer isn't working. If you let me know a different bank account number, I'll send it there.
Hyunsoo	Sure, then send it to this account.
	Seoul Bank 1002-678-947365
Mael	Sent. Please check. Thank you.

얼마 나왔어?

When checking the total amount that the food cost at a restaurant, 얼마야? is also used, but a more commonly used expression is 얼마 나왔어?. It is also more natural to answer by saying 3만 원 나왔어 rather than 3만 원이야.

- **A: 얼마 나왔어?** How much was it?
  B: 3만 원 나왔어. It was 30,000 won.

`NS` `IL`

N빵

N빵 means that when multiple people gather for a meal or prepare a gift together, the total cost is divided by the number of people. The reason why the number of people is written as N is because in mathematics, N is used to represent an unknown or undetermined number. Even in situations where the number of people is fixed, it is written as N빵 (read as 엔빵) or 1/N (read as 엔분의 일). Rather than having each person pay for what they ate, one person pays with a card at the restaurant, and then the others send their share of the cost to that person later through a bank transfer or KakaoTalk's settlement function.

- **일단 내가 계산할게. 나중에 N빵하자.** I'll pay for now. Let's settle up later.

- **N빵해서 친구 생일 선물 사 주자.**
  Let's split the cost and buy a birthday present for our friend.

- **정산 좀 부탁해. N분의 1한 금액을 알려 줘.**
  Please calculate the cost. Let me know the amount each person should pay.

N 을/를 N빵하다

1차

In Korea, gatherings usually take place somewhere outside, not at home. First you eat a meal at a restaurant, then you go to somewhere else like a café or bar. Every time you move to a different location, it is expressed with 1차, 2차, 3차 etc.

- 밥은 다 먹었고, 우리 2차는 어디로 갈까?
  We've finished our food. Where should we go for round 2?

- 오늘 좀 힘들어서 난 1차만 하고 집에 갈게.
  I'm a bit tired today, so I'm only going to the first round and then going home.

Quick Check

Contacting People

■ to send a text message	문자 (메시지)를 보내다
■ to receive a text message	문자 (메시지)를 받다
■ to use KaTalk	카톡을 하다
■ to send a Katalk message	톡을 보내다
■ the KaTalk message does not arrive	톡이 [1]안 오 다
■ to make a group chat	단톡방을 만들다
■ to invite a friend to a group chat	단톡방에 친구를 [2]▨ ▨ ▨
■ to leave a group chat	단톡방에서 [3]▨ ▨ ▨

Searching for and Deciding on a Place to Meet

■ to search for a place on the internet	인터넷에서/으로 장소를 검색하다
■ to send / leave a link, to link (to something)	링크를 보내다 / 남기다 / 걸다
■ to share a link	링크를 [4]▨ ▨ ▨ ▨
■ to check a link	링크를 확인하다
■ to click and follow a link	링크를 눌러서 들어가다
■ to make a poll in a group chat	단톡방에 투표를 [5]▨ ▨ ▨

1 안 오다 2 초대하다 3 나가다 4 공유하다 5 올리다

■ to vote	투표를 하다
■ Friday gets the most votes	금요일이 많이 ¹▢▢▢

Making Reservations

■ to make a reservation at a restaurant under the name Park Yuna	박유나 이름으로 식당을 예약하다
■ to reserve a window seat / terrace / private room	창가 / 테라스 / 개별 룸으로 예약하다
■ a reservation is confirmed	예약이 ²▢▢▢▢
■ to share a reservation confirmation message	예약 확인 문자를 공유하다
■ there are no seats available on Friday	금요일에는 ³▢▢▢▢
■ reservations are fully booked	예약이 ⁴▢ ▢▢
■ to put one's name on a waiting list	대기자 명단 / 대기 리스트에 이름을 ⁵▢▢▢
■ to link a map	지도 링크를 ⁶▢▢
■ to find one's way by looking at a map	지도를 보고 잘 찾아오다
■ to change the reservation day to Saturday	예약 날짜를 토요일로 바꾸다 / ⁷▢▢▢▢
■ to cancel a reservation	예약을 취소하다

1 나오다 2 확정되다 3 만석이다 4 다 차다 5 올리다 6 걸다 7 변경하다

At the Restaurant

- to wait a moment before being shown to one's seat / table

  자리를 안내할 때까지 잠깐 기다리다

- to sit wherever you'd like

  편한 자리에 앉다

- all the seats are full

  자리가 다 차다

- to have no tables for three people

  세 명 자리가 없다

- a seat is open

  자리가¹

- to choose what to eat

  메뉴를 고르다

- to ask someone to recommend what to eat

  메뉴를 추천해 달라고 하다

- to order food

  음식을 시키다 / 주문하다

- to press the bell

  벨을 누르다

- a buzzer vibrates

  진동 벨이 울리다

- the food that was ordered is ready

  주문한 음식이 나오다

- to go get the food

  음식을²

- the food hasn't come out yet

  밥이³

- to have garlic in the food

  음식에 마늘이 들어가 있다

- to order one additional serving

  1인분 더 추가로 주문하다

- "Please give us individual plates."

  "개인 접시 좀 주세요."

1 나다 2 가지러 가다 3 아직 안 나오다

■ to pack up leftover food	¹ ▨▨ ▨▨을 싸다 / 포장하다

Paying and Settling up

■ to pay the cost of the food with a credit card / cash	음식값을 카드 / 현금으로 계산하다
■ to send a bank transfer for the cost of the food	음식값을 ²▨▨ ▨▨▨▨
■ "Please place your phone here."	"핸드폰을 여기에 대 주세요."
■ "Please insert your card here."	"카드를 여기에 ³▨▨ ▨▨▨"
■ "Please sign here."	"여기에 ⁴▨▨▨ ▨▨▨".
■ "Please throw away the receipt."	"영수증은 버려 주세요"
■ to pay individually	각자 계산하다
■ to pay all at once first and settle up later	일단 한꺼번에 계산하고 나중에 ⁵▨▨▨▨
■ to request a settlement	정산을 요청하다
■ to let someone know one's bank account number	계좌 번호를 알려 주다
■ to send a wire transfer to this account	이 계좌로 ⁶▨▨ ▨▨▨

1 남은 음식   2 계좌 이체하다   3 꽂아 주세요   4 서명해 주세요   5 정산하다   6 송금하다

■	to send a wire transfer	송금을 보내다
■	to receive a wire transfer	송금을 받다
■	the wire transfer (doesn't) work	송금이 (¹)

1 (안) 되다

7

행복해지고 싶다면 떠나라

If You Want to Be Happier, Leave

Before Reaching the Destination

Vocabulary

가 볼 만한 곳을 검색하다
to search for a place worth going to

부산에 2박 3일로 여행 가다
to go on a 2-night, 3-day trip to Busan

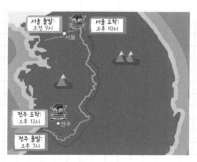

전주에 당일치기로 갔다 오다
to go on a day trip to Jeonju

동선이 꼬이다
the travel path is complicated

거기로 가는 교통편이 불편하다
transportation to get there is inconvenient

자동차를 렌트하다
to rent a car

073

① 계획 / 일정 / 동선을 짜다
to make a plan / schedule / travel path

여행 가기 전에 대충이라도 일정을 짜 두는 게 어때?
How about we at least roughly make a schedule before we go on a trip?

② 교통편을 알아보다
to look into transportation

교통편을 알아보고 제일 빠른 걸로 이용하자.
Let's look into transportation and use the fastest method.

③ 중간에 한 번 갈아타다 / 환승하다
to transfer once in the middle

거기는 바로 가는 버스가 없어서 중간에 한 번 갈아타야 돼.
There aren't any buses that go directly there, so we have to transfer once in the middle.

④ 버스 / 기차를 놓치다
to miss the bus / train

역으로 가는 길이 너무 막혀서 기차를 놓쳤어.
Traffic was really backed up on the way to the station, so I missed my train.

⑤ 부산에서 렌트해서 다니다
to rent a car to go around Busan

부산은 크니까 부산에서 여행할 때는 렌트해서 다니는 게 편해.
Busan is large, so renting a car to go around while traveling there is convenient.

⑥ 짐을 싸다
to pack one's luggage

오늘 저녁에는 짐을 꼭 싸야 하는데 많이 귀찮네.
I have to make sure to pack my luggage this evening, but it's so bothersome.

Dialogue

Tips

★**흩어져 있다** to be scattered

★**몇 군데** multiple places

Yuna   I searched for places that are worth visiting in Busan, and they're spread out all over the place.

Ryo   There are multiple places I want to go to as well, but there isn't a bus that goes directly there.

Alex   Then how about renting a car to get around? I'll drive.

Yuna   Oh, that would be great. I can take turns driving with you.

074

Tips

★대신 instead

Ing   Okay, then since we are going there, let's go everywhere we want to go.

Ryo   I can't drive···. but instead, I'll work hard on all the general affairs.

돌아가면서 운전하면 되잖아.

This expression means that rather than one person continuously driving, other people will also determine an order to take turns driving. 돌아가면서 means that multiple people take turns doing something instead of one person continuously doing it alone.

- **돌아가면서 청소하자.** Let's take turns cleaning.

- **돌아가면서 점심을 사는 게 어때?** How about we take turns buying lunch?

- **가전제품이 돌아가면서 고장 나서 정신이 없네.**
  I'm losing my mind because my home appliances are taking turns breaking down.

돌아가면서

이왕 가는 거 우리 가고 싶은 데 다 가자.

이왕 means "since a matter has already been decided" or "since a situation has already occurred." It is mainly used in the form 이왕 V는 거. And after 이왕 V는 거, there should be expressions or contents related to the best choice that can be done in that situation.

- **이왕 먹는 거 맛있는 걸로 먹자.**
  Since we're eating anyway, let's eat something delicious.

- **이왕 하는 거 재미있게 잘하고 싶어.**
  Since I'm already doing it, I want to do it well and have fun.

- **이왕 사는 거 예쁜 걸로 살래.**
  Since I'm going to buy something, I want to buy something pretty.

이왕 V는 거

075

총무

In an institution or organization, 총무 refers to a department or person in charge of overall general affairs. With this as its origin, the word 총무 is used in social gatherings as well. The person designated as 총무 in social gatherings is usually in charge of contacting people and managing membership fees. When traveling, 총무 is responsible for paying at hotels, restaurants, cafés, etc. and then making sure everyone settles up later. It is used in the forms 총무를 하다(to handle general affairs such as paying or calculating costs), 총무를 맡다(to take on general affairs).

● A: 누가 총무할래?
　　Who wants to be in charge of general affairs?

　B: 총무는 돌아가면서 하자.
　　Let's take turns handling the general affairs.

2

At the Accommodation

Vocabulary

숙소에서 짐을 풀다
to unpack one's luggage at their accommodation

부대 시설을 이용하다
to use facilities

조식을 먹다
to eat breakfast

카드 키를 대고 문을 열다
to touch a key card (to the lock panel) and open the door

카드 키를 꽂고 불을 켜다
to insert a key card and turn on the lights

입실 / 퇴실 시간을 안내하다
to inform the check-in / check-out time

숙소에 체크인하다
to check in to one's accommodation

숙소에 짐을 맡기다
to leave one's luggage at their accommodation

① 뷰가 좋은 방 / 높은 층 / 조용한 방으로 받다
to receive a room with a good view / a room on a high floor / a quiet room

조용한 방으로 받아서 편하게 쉴 수 있었어.
I received a quiet room, so I was able to rest comfortably.

② 숙소에 짐을 내려놓다
to drop off one's luggage at their accommodation

숙소에 짐만 내려놓고 바로 나가자.
Let's just drop off our luggage at our accommodation and then go out.

③ 룸 서비스를 시키다
to order room service

아침은 룸 서비스를 시켜서 편하게 먹고 싶어.
I want to order room service for breakfast and eat comfortably.

④ 휴지가 다 떨어지다
to run out of toilet paper

휴지가 다 떨어졌어요. 휴지 좀 갖다주세요.
We've run out of toilet paper. Please bring us some more.

⑤ 물이 잘 안 나오다
the water doesn't come out well

이 방은 물이 잘 안 나와요. 다른 방으로 바꿔 주세요.
The water doesn't come out well in this room. Please move us to a different room.

Dialogue

Mom   My daughter, did you arrive safely?

Yuna   Yes, Mom. I just checked in and entered my room.

Mom   How's your room? Is it okay?

Yuna   It has a totally amazing view. Look over here. The night view is insane. I seriously can't wait to see how it looks in the morning.

Mom   Wow, it's really great. Take a lot of pictures. What are you going to do now? Have you eaten dinner?

Yuna   Not yet.

Yuna   Now I'm going to unpack and order room service.

Mom   Okay, enjoy your dinner and have fun on your trip.

이제 막

이제 막 is an expression that means right now as it is being said, emphasizing that it has only been a short time since something happened.

- **이제 막 출발했어.** I just departed.

- **이제 막 끝났어.** We just finished.

- **이제 막 시작했어.** It just started.

NS **BW**

뷰 맛집

맛집 means a restaurant with delicious food. This has expanded to be used when describing not only restaurants, but other places that do something well or places where something is great. 뷰 맛집 means a place with a great view.

- **분위기 맛집** a restaurant / café / lodging with a good atmosphere

- **가성비 맛집** a place / brand with good value compared to price

- **댓글 맛집** a post with funny comments

078

아침에는 어떨지 완전 기대돼요.

When expressing that you are waiting for something good to happen even though you cannot know for sure that it will happen, the expression A/V 을지 기대되다 is used combined with an interrogative word.

- **어떤 일을 하게 될지 기대돼.**
  I can't wait to see what kind of work you'll do.

- **내년에 어디로 여행 갈지 기대돼.**
  I can't wait to see where we travel next year.

- **얼마나 많은 사람들이 올지 기대돼.**
  I'm excited to see how many people will come.

interrogative A/V 을지 기대되다

3

At a Must-Eat Place

Vocabulary

줄 Lines

- **줄을 서다** to stand in line
- **줄을 서서 기다리다** to stand and wait in line
- **대기줄이 길다** the waiting line is long

월요일은 휴무이다
to be closed on Mondays

세 시에 브레이크 타임이 시작되다
break time starts at 3:00

다섯 시에 브레이크 타임이 끝나다
break time ends at 5:00

대기 리스트 Waitlist

- **대기 리스트에 이름을 올리다**
  to put one's name on a waitlist
- **대기 리스트에 연락처를 남기다**
  to leave one's phone number
  on a waitlist

079

① 현지인들이 자주 가는 맛집
a good restaurant that is frequented by locals

A: 여행 왔는데 이왕이면 여기에서 제일 맛있는 걸 먹어 보고 싶어.
　　While I'm here on a trip, I want to eat the most delicious food possible.

B: 여기가 현지인들이 자주 가는 맛집이래. 이런 곳이 찐이야. 여기로 가자.
　　I heard that this is a great restaurant that is frequented by locals. This kind of place is the real deal. Let's go here.

② 차례가 되다 to be one's turn

A: 우리 차례 언제 오는 거야? 기다리기 힘들다.
　　When will it be our turn? It's so tiring to wait.

B: 드디어 우리 차례가 됐어. 들어가자.
　　It's finally our turn. Let's go in.

③ 김치만두가 품절되다 Kimchi dumplings are sold out

A: 김치만두 2인분 주세요.
　　Please give us two servings of Kimchi dumplings.

B: 김치만두는 품절됐는데, 고기만두는 어떠세요?
　　The Kimchi dumplings are all sold out. How about meat dumplings?

④ 재료가 다 떨어지다 / 소진되다 to run out of ingredients

A: 죄송합니다. 오늘 준비된 재료가 다 소진됐어요.
　　I'm sorry. We ran out of all the ingredients we prepared for today.

B: 아, 그럼 먹을 수 없는 거예요? 오래 기다렸는데…….
　　Oh, so we can't eat here? But we waited for so long….

⑤ 아홉 시가 주문 마감 시간이다 last order is at 9:00

A: 아홉 시가 주문 마감 시간이에요. 더 필요한 거 있으면 지금 알려 주세요.
　　Last order is at 9:00. If you need anything else, please let me know now.

B: 그럼 치킨 반 마리 추가로 주문할게요.
　　Then we'll order another half chicken, please.

Dialogue

Alex   Just look at that waiting line. Is this for real?

080

Yuna   I put my name on the waitlist, but there are more than 20 groups on the list.

Ing   Dang! Then how long do we have to wait?

Yuna   I asked, and they said it will take about two hours.

Ryo   If we spend that much time here, our schedule will get all messed up. What should we do?

Alex   Agh, this is no good. Let's just go somewhere else.

Ing   Yeah. I'll quickly search for a good restaurant nearby.

BW

실화

실화 means a "true story," not a fictional story or a novel. Recently, this expression has come to be used as an expression of one's disbelief upon seeing or hearing something amazing. It is usually used in the forms 이거 실화냐?, 이거 실화임?

- **시험 2일 남은 거 실화냐?**
  Do we really have 2 days of exams left?

- **핸드폰을 사면 무선 이어폰을 같이 준다고? 이거 실화임?**
  If I buy a phone, I get wireless earphones for free? Is this for real?

- **두 달 동안 열심히 운동했는데, 몸무게가 똑같다니, 이거 실화냐?**
  I exercised hard for two months, but my weight is still the same. Seriously?

이거 실화냐?

일정이 다 꼬이는데 어떡하냐?

어떡하냐 is short for 어떻게 하냐, and is commonly used to initiate discussions on how to deal with a problem or simply to express worries or concerns. It is often used in forms such as 어떡해?, 어떡하지?. It is connected with A/V은/는데 to explain the problematic situation.

- **예약이 다 찼다는데 어떡해?**
  They said that their reservations are fully booked. What should we do?

- **배터리가 다 나갔는데 어떡하냐?** My battery is dead. Now what?

081

● 걔를 더 기다리다가는 기차를 놓치는데 어떡하지?

If we wait for him any longer, we're going to miss my train. What should we do?

A/V 는데 어떡하냐? / 어떡해? / 어떡하지?

BW

이건 좀 아니지.

When you feel that something doesn't seem right or you do not like it, and you can use 이건 좀 아니다 to oppose it and point out the problems with the current situation. By adding 이건 좀 아니지, 이건 좀 아닌 것 같아, 이건 좀 아니지 않아?, you can emphasize the content of your protest regarding the specific complaint.

● 이건 좀 아닌 것 같아. 예약하고 왔는데 한 시간을 기다리래.

This doesn't seem right. We made a reservation and came here, but they said we have to wait for one hour.

● 이렇게 갑자기 약속을 취소해? 아, 이건 좀 아니지 않아?

You're suddenly canceling our appointment? Hey, this isn't right, is it?

● 새로 산 지 일주일 만에 고장 난 핸드폰. 이건 좀 아니지.

My new phone broke only one week after I bought it. This just isn't right.

이건 좀 아니다

4

Taking and Sharing Photos

Vocabulary

바다가 나오게 찍다
to take a picture with the ocean in it

사진이 분위기 있게 나오다
a photo turns out with a certain vibe

얼굴만 나오게 찍다
to take a picture only showing your face(s)

구도가 좋다
to be well composed

역광이라서 어둡게 나오다
to come out dark due to being backlit

사진이 잘 나오다
a photo turns out well

082

① 셀카 / 동영상 / 단체 사진을 찍다
to take a selfie / video / group picture

혼자 여행을 가서 셀카를 많이 찍었어.
I traveled alone, so I took a lot of selfies.

② 타이머를 맞춰 놓고 찍다 to set a timer and take a picture

타이머를 맞춰 놓고 찍었는데 포즈가 좀 이상하지?
I set a timer and took this picture, but the pose is a bit weird, right?

③ 사진을 찍어 달라고 부탁하다 to ask someone to take a picture

우리 저 사람한테 사진 찍어 달라고 부탁할까?
Shall we ask that person over there to take a picture for us?

④ 프사 각이다 to be fit for a profile picture

와! 이 사진 대박이다. 완전 프사 각이야.
Wow! This photo is amazing. It's totally fit for a profile picture.

⑤ 사진이 흔들리다 the photo is shaky

사진이 다 흔들려서 쓸 만한 게 없어.
The photos are all shaky, so none of them are worth using.

⑥ 사진이 초점이 안 맞다 the photo is out of focus

이 사진 초점이 안 맞아. 우리 얼굴은 흐릿하고 앞에 있는 꽃이 선명하게 나왔어.
This photo is out of focus. Our faces are blurry and the flowers in front of us came out clear.

⑦ 사진을 보정하다 to touch up a photo

사진은 찍는 것보다 보정하는 게 더 중요해.
Touching up photos is more important than how you take them.

⑧ 보정으로 밝게 하다 to use photoshop to brighten a photo

사진이 어둡게 나와서 보정으로 밝게 했는데, 어때?
The photo came out dark, so I used photoshop to brighten it. How does it look?

⑨ 보정으로 다른 사람들을 지우다 / 없애다
to use photoshop to remove other people

보정으로 다른 사람들을 없앨 수 있을까?
Could we photoshop to remove other people?

Dialogue

Ing   This place is so pretty. Should we all take a group photo together? We gotta have proof picture that we went here.

Yuna   Shall we ask that person over there to take a picture for us?

Ryo   I think we can just set a timer and take it ourselves.

Alex   Yeah. I'll set up the camera so the ocean and bridge both show up and then start the timer.

083

Tips

*표정 expression

Yuna   Please share the picture you took earlier in our group chat.

Ryo   The composition and our expressions are perfect, but the photo isn't quite right since there are other people next to us.

Ing   Just a second. I'll try to erase them.

Ing   What do you think? Looks totally natural, right?

Alex   Haha, you did an awesome job with photoshop.

NS

인증 샷

인증 샷 combines 인증 with the English word "shot" written in Korean alphabet as 샷. It refers to a photo taken to prove or boast about having done something. It usually ends with posting the photo on one's social media. 샷 is combined with other words to be used in a variety of ways.

- **항공샷**

  When taking photos of food, the picture is usually taken from high up, like an airplane, so the entire table is visible

- **거울샷**

  A photo of oneself reflected in a mirror

- **인생샷**

  A very cool photo that you will remember for a long time in your life.

N 샷

084

딱

딱 is an adverb that means something fits exactly and perfectly. It is also used in the form N이/가 딱이다 to mean that something fits 100% well or is 100% great.

● **가격이나 위치를 보면 이 호텔이 딱이야.**
Considering the price and location, this hotel is perfect.

● **이 옷이 너한테 딱인데 사이즈가 없어.**
This piece of clothing suits you perfectly, but they don't have your size.

● **여기가 딱이야.** This place is just right.

N **이/가 딱이다**

좀 그렇다.

N이/가 좀 그렇다 is used when one doesn't really like something or when one disagrees with an opinion. You can express denial or rejection in a more gentle way by saying this without specifying the reason.

● **여긴 좀 그래. 다른 곳으로 알아보자.**
This place isn't quite right. Let's look for a different place.

● **이 호텔은 시설은 좋은데 서비스는 좀 그렇더라.**
This hotel has good facilities, but the service isn't up to par.

● **그 사람하고 같이 만나는 건 좀 그런데…….**
Meeting with that person is a bit awkward….

N **이/가 좀 그렇다**

Making Travel Plans

- to search for a place worth going to

  가 볼 만한 곳을 검색하다

- to make a plan / schedule / travel path

  계획 / 일정 / 동선을 [1] 짜 다

- to go on a 2-night, 3-day trip to Busan

  부산에 2박 3일로 여행 가다

- to go on a day trip to Jeonju

  전주에 당일치기로 갔다 오다

Luggage

- to pack one's luggage

  짐을 [2]

- to drop off one's luggage at their accommodation

  숙소에 짐을 내려놓다

- to unpack one's luggage at their accommodation

  숙소에서 짐을 [3]

- to leave one's luggage at their accommodation

  숙소에 짐을 [4]

- to carry one's luggage around

  짐을 들고 다니다

---

1 짜다 2 싸다 3 풀다 4 맡기다

Using Transportation

- to look into transportation

  교통편을 알아보다

- transportation to get there is inconvenient

  거기로 가는 교통편이 불편하다

- to transfer once in the middle

  중간에 한 번 갈아타다 /

  ¹▨▨▨▨

- to rent a car

  자동차를 렌트하다

- to rent a car to go around Busan

  부산에서 렌트해서 다니다

At the Accommodation

- to check in to one's accommodation

  숙소에 체크인하다

- to inform the check-in / check-out time

  ²▨▨ / ▨▨ 시간을 안내하다

- to receive a room with a good view / a room on a high floor / a quiet room

  뷰가 좋은 방 / 높은 층 / 조용한 방으로 받다

- to touch a key card (to the lock panel) and open the door

  카드 키를 ³▨▨ 문을 열다

- to insert a key card and turn on the lights

  카드 키를 ⁴▨▨ 불을 켜다

- to order room service

  룸 서비스를 시키다

- to eat breakfast

  조식을 먹다

1 환승하다 2 입실, 퇴실 3 대고 4 꽂고

■	to use facilities	부대 시설을 이용하다
■	to run out of toilet paper	휴지가 [1]
■	the water doesn't come out well	물이 [2]

Problems Arise

■	the travel path / schedule is complicated	동선 / 일정이 [3]
■	to miss the bus / train	버스 / 기차를 [4]
■	to leave one's hat on the bus	버스에 모자를 놓고 내리다

At a Restaurant with Delicious Food

■	a good restaurant that is frequented by locals	현지인들이 자주 가는 맛집
■	to stand in line	줄을 서다
■	to stand and wait in line	줄을 서서 기다리다
■	the waiting line is long	[5] 이 길다
■	to put one's name on a waitlist	대기 리스트에 이름을 올리다
■	to leave one's phone number on a waitlist	대기 리스트에 연락처를 남기다
■	to be one's turn	[6] 가 되다

1 다 떨어지다 2 잘 안 나오다 3 꼬이다 4 놓치다 5 대기 줄 6 차례

■ Kimchi dumplings are sold out	김치만두가 [1] ▨▨▨▨
■ to run out of ingredients	재료가 다 떨어지다 / 소진되다
■ to be closed on Mondays	월요일은 [2] ▨▨▨
■ break time starts at 3:00	세 시에 브레이크 타임이 시작되다
■ break time ends at 5:00	다섯 시에 브레이크 타임이 끝나다
■ last order is at 9:00	아홉 시가 주문 마감 시간이다

Taking Photos

■ to take a selfie / video / group picture	셀카 / 동영상 / 단체 사진을 찍다
■ to take a picture with the ocean in it	바다가 [3] ▨▨▨ ▨▨
■ to take a picture only showing your face(s)	얼굴만 나오게 찍다
■ to set a timer and take a picture	타이머를 맞춰 놓고 찍다
■ to ask someone to take a picture	사진을 [4] ▨▨▨ ▨▨ 부탁하다
■ a photo turns out well	사진이 [5] ▨▨ ▨▨▨
■ a photo turns out with a certain vibe	사진이 분위기 있게 나오다
■ to be well composed	구도가 좋다

1 품절되다 2 휴무다 3 나오게 찍다 4 찍어 달라고 5 잘 나오다

- to be fit for a profile picture　　　프사 각이다

- the photo is shaky　　　사진이 [1] ▢ ▢ ▢

- the photo is out of focus　　　사진이 [2] ▢ ▢ ▢ ▢ ▢ ▢

- to come out dark due to being backlit　　　역광이라서 어둡게 나오다

Touching Up Photos

- to touch up a photo　　　사진을 보정하다

- to use photoshop to brighten a photo　　　보정으로 사진을 밝게 하다

- to use photoshop to remove other people　　　보정으로 다른 사람들을 [3] ▢ ▢ ▢ / ▢ ▢ ▢

---

1 흔들리다　2 초점이 안 맞다　3 지우다, 없애다

Appendix

Korean Translation

1. 핸드폰을 새로 샀다
I Bought a New Cell Phone!

---

1   New Cell Phone

Dialogue

Tips

신상: '신상품'의 줄임말

그지?: '그렇지?'의 줄임말로 그지는 어법적으로 잘못된 표현이나 대화에서는 그지, 그치의 형태로 많이 사용된다.

맘: '마음'의 줄임말이다.

근데: '그런데'의 줄임말이다.

Expressions

비/유 **대박!**

'대박'은 원래 큰 성공이라는 뜻으로 '대박이 나다'라고 하면 큰 성공을 하다라는 뜻이다. 최근에는 여기에서 의미가 확장되어 놀랍다, 좋다, 혹은 대단하다는 의미의 감탄사로 사용된다. 부사로 사용되면 아주라는 뜻으로 뒤에 오는 말을 강조한다. '대박, 대박이다'의 형태로 사용된다.

실물로 보니 더 예쁜데?

'실물로 보다'는 사진이나 화면으로 본 사람이나 물건을 실제로 봤다는 뜻으로, '실물로 보니(까)' 다음에는 그것을 실제로 봤을 때 느낀 점이나 새로 알게 된 점 등을 쓰면 된다.

유 **카메라 화질이 장난 아니야.**

'장난 아니다'는 농담이 아니다, 진지하다라는 의미이다. 여기에서 의미가 확장되어 엄청나게 좋다 혹은 정도가 아주 심하다는 의미로도 사용한다. 동사나 형용사 앞에는 부사 형태로 '장난 아니게'를 사용한다.

비/유/속 **색감도 쩔어.**

'쩔다'는 어떤 것이 아주 좋다, 멋있다, 엄청나다 등의 의미이며 '쩔어, 쩐다' 등의 형태로 사용된다. 비속어이므로 사용에 주의가 필요하다.

---

2   Using a Cell Phone

Expressions

비/유 **헐!**

'헐!'은 놀라거나 어이없는 상황에서 사용되는 감탄사이다. 비격식적인 표현이므로 사용에 주의해야 한다.

잘못 입력한 거 아니야?

'잘못 입력한 거 아니야?'는 질문이 아니라 사실상 잘못 입력한 것 같다는 뜻이다. 이처럼 'A/V은/는 거 아니야?'를 이용하면 자신의 생각을 질문의 형태로 부드럽게 돌려서 표현할 수 있다.

g가 아니라 9네.

'(A는) B가 아니라 C예요'는 'A는 B가 아니에요. A는 C예요'를 줄인 표현이다.

개

'그 아이'의 줄임말이며 보통 친구나 자기보다 나이가 어린 사람을 지칭할 때 사용한다. '얘'는 이 아이, '쟤'는 저 아이의 줄임말이다.

---

3   Using an App

Expressions

(일정이) 많다기보다는 헷갈려.

'많다기보다는 헷갈려'는 일정이 많은 것이 아니라 헷갈린다는 뜻이다. 'A/V다기보다는'에 비교를 나타내는 조사인 '보다'가 포함되어 있지만, 앞뒤 내용을 비교하는 것이 아니라 사실상 앞의 내용을 부드럽게 부정하면서 뒤의 내용이 더 적절하다는 것을 나타내는 표현이다.

그날그날 달라서 헷갈려.

'그날그날 다르다'는 어떤 것이 고정되어 있지 않고 날마다 다르다는 뜻이다.

한눈에 보여서 훨씬 좋네.

'한눈'이란 눈으로 한 번에 볼 수 있는 범위를 뜻하며 '한눈에 보이다'는 한 번만 봐도 전체가 쉽게 파악된다는 의미이다. '한눈에 볼 수 있다. 한눈에 들어오다'의 형태로도 사용된다.

4   Cell Phone Problems

Dialogue

톡을 보내다

'톡'은 한국에서 가장 많이 사용되는 메신저 앱인 '카카오톡'의 줄임말이며, '톡을 보내다'는 카카오톡으로 메시지를 보냈다는 말이다.

Expressions

톡을 몇 번이나 보냈는데 확인도 안 하고.

'몇 번이나 V았/었는데'는 어떤 행동을 여러 번 자주 했음을 강조할 때 사용한다. V았/었는데 다음에는, 예상했던 것과 다른 결과가 나온다. 따라서 이 표현에는 실망이나 짜증, 혹은 화의 감정이 담겨있다.

오래돼서 그런가?

'A/V아/어서 그런가?'는 어떤 결과가 생긴 것이 혹시 이 이유 때문일까 생각해 보며 말할 때 사용한다. 질문의 형태이지만 상대방의 대답을 요하는 것은 아니다.

유 **보내 줄 때도 됐네.**

'보내 주다'는 원래 자유롭게 떠날 수 있게 해 주다라는 의미이다. 어떤 물건을 '보내 줄 때도 됐다'라고 하면 그 물건이 오래돼서 이제 그만 사용하거나 버려야겠다는 뜻이다.

1 Starting to Use Instagram

Dialogue

Tips

최애: 가장 사랑하는 대상이라는 뜻으로 보통 아이돌 그룹에서 자신이 제일 좋아하는 멤버를 가리킬 때 많이 사용한다.
라방: '라이브 방송'의 줄임말
인스타: '인스타그램'의 줄임말

Expressions

답글 남겨 줄지 누가 알아?
'누가 알아?'는 어떤 일이 어떻게 일어날지 아무도 알 수 없다는 뜻으로, 가능성이 적어 보여도 전혀 없지는 않다고 말할 때 쓰는 표현이다. 앞에 'A/V을지'를 써서 'A/V을지 누가 알아?'의 형태로 많이 쓴다.

댓글이 얼마나 많은데 내 거 읽기나 하겠어?
'댓글이 얼마나 많은데'는 댓글이 아주 많다는 것을 강조하는 표현이며, '읽기나 하겠어?'는 읽을 가능성이 전혀 없다는 것을 질문의 형식으로 표현한 것이다. 따라서 이는 댓글이 너무 많아서 자기 댓글은 읽을 리가 없다는 뜻이다. 이와 같이 '얼마나 많은데 V기나 하겠어?'는 어떤 것이 너무 많아서 그 일이 일어날 가능성이 거의 없을 때 쓸 수 있다.

적당히 해라.
'적당히'는 지나치지 않게 정도에 알맞게라는 뜻으로, '적당히 해라'는 너무 지나치니까 그만하라는 표현이다. 선을 넘지 말고 적정선을 지켜서 행동하라는 조언이나 경고가 된다.

그러다가 차단당한다.
'그러다가 차단당한다'는 앞 문장의 행동을 계속하면 차단당하는 나쁜 결과로 이어질 수 있음을 경고하는 의미다. '그러다가(는)'는 앞선 행동을 계속하면 나쁜 결과가 생길 수 있다는 뜻으로, 경고하거나 그 행동을 그만 하라고 조언할 때 사용한다.

2 Instagram Posts

Dialogue

Tips

집사: 원래 butler(집사)라는 뜻인데 고양이를 키우는 사람들 사이에서 고양이 주인이라는 뜻으로도 쓰인다.

Expressions

비/속 **멍 때려도 귀여워.**
'멍하다'는 아무 생각 없이 정신이 나간 상태를 의미한다. '멍 때리다'는 멍하게 있다의 비속어로 사용에 주의가 필요하다. 이와 관련해서 불을 보면서 멍 때리다는 '불멍', 물을 보면서 멍 때리다는 '물멍'이라는 신조어도 만들어졌는데 불이나 물을 보면서 아무 생각없이 편하게 쉬면서 힐링한다는 의미를 포함하고 있다.

어쩜 이래?

'어쩜'은 '어쩌면'의 줄임말이며 '어쩜 이래?'
는 어떤 것을 보면서 믿을 수 없을 정도로
좋다, 맛있다, 귀엽다라고 말하고 싶을 때
사용하는 감탄사이다.

안 예쁜 데가 하나도 없네.

부정어 '안'과 '하나도 없다'가 같이 쓰이면
강한 긍정의 의미를 지닌다. 따라서 '안 예
쁜 데가 하나도 없네'는 모든 곳이 다 예쁘
다는 뜻이다.

비 심쿵

'심장이 쿵 내려앉다, 쿵쿵 뛰다'는 부정적인
상황에서 놀랐을 때 사용하는 표현이다. 여
기에서 '심쿵'이 유래했는데 원래의 뜻과는
달리 너무 귀엽거나 멋있는 것을 보고 마음
을 뺏기거나 설렐 때 사용한다. '심쿵' 혹은
'심쿵하다'의 형태로 사용할 수 있다.

....

3 Using Instagram

....

Dialogue

Tips

본격: 원래는 '본격적으로'가 맞는 표현이다.
냥스타 그램: 고양이 사진을 올리는 인스타
그램의 피드나 계정

Expressions

비 짱

'정말, 아주'의 의미로 보통 긍정적인 의미의
형용사와 같이 써서 그 형용사를 강조할 때

사용된다.

좋아요 수가 폭발이거든.

'폭발'은 원래 힘이나 기운이 갑자기 퍼지거
나 세지는 모습을 뜻하므로 '수가 폭발이다'
라고 하면 수가 갑자기 많아졌다는 것을 의
미한다.

유 반전 매력

'반전'은 사건이나 일의 흐름이 뒤바뀌는 것
을 의미하며 보통 영화나 소설 등에서 많이
사용된다. '반전 매력'은 평소에 보여지던 모
습과 반대인 모습이 나왔을 때 주는 뜻밖의
매력이라는 뜻이다.

유 루돌프 귀여운 거 세상 사람들 다 알아
야지.

'세상 사람들 다 알아야지'는 너무 좋아서 많
은 사람들이 다 알았으면 좋겠다, 많은 사람
들에게 알려 주고 싶다는 의미로 사용한다.
'세상 사람들 다 알아야 돼'의 형태로도 사용
된다.

....

4 Using YouTube

....

Expressions

뭐 생각해 놓은 거 있어?

이 표현은 계획이나 아이디어가 있는지를
물어보는 표현으로 여기에서 '뭐'는 의문사
가 아니라 '뭔가'의 줄임 말로 정확하게 지
칭되지 않은 어떤 것의 의미를 갖는다.

아무나 하는 거 아니다.

이는 보기에는 쉬워 보여도 절대 누구나 쉽게 할 수 있는 일이 아니다라는 의미의 표현이다.

어떻게든 되겠지.

이 표현은 어떤 일에 대한 구체적인 방안이나 대책이 없이 막연히 낙관적으로 어떤 식으로든 진행될 거라고 전망할 때 사용한다. 무책임하게 들릴 수 있으므로 사용에 주의해야 한다.

3. 인터넷만 보면 다 사고 싶어
I Want to Buy Everything I See on the Internet

1   Online Shopping

Vocabulary

> **Tips**

신상: '신상품'의 줄임말

Dialogue

> **Tips**

니: '네'의 비격식적 표현
지르다: '사다'의 속어

Expressions

이거 살까 말까?

'이거 살까 말까?'는 '살까? 사지 말까?'를 줄여서 표현한 것으로, 어떤 것을 살지 말지

고민하고 있을 때 사용할 수 있다. 'V을까 말까?'는 어떤 일을 할지 하지 않을지 고민하는 상황에서, 어떤 선택을 하는 것이 좋을지 다른 이에게 조언을 구할 때 사용하는 표현이다.

몇 주째 고민만 하고 있어.

이는 몇 주 동안 고민만 하면서 아무 것도 하고 있지 않을 때 쓸 수 있다. 'N만 V고 있다'는 뒤따라야 하는 행위를 이어하지 않고 그 상황에만 장시간 계속 머물러 있을 때 쓴다. '몇 주째, 며칠째, 몇 시간째, 몇 분째' 등과 사용할 수 있다.

비 **열일**

이는 '열심히'와 '일하다'가 합쳐진 신조어로 '열일, 열일하다' 등으로 쓰인다. 비슷한 표현으로는 '열심히'와 '공부하다'가 합쳐진 '열공'이 있다.

유 **빨리 사서 자주 하고 다니는 게 남는 거야.**

'자주 하고 다니다'는 많이 사용한다는 뜻이고, '남다'는 이익이 된다는 뜻이다. 따라서 위 문장은 살지 말지 고민되는 상황에서 어차피 사게 될 거라면 망설이지 말고 얼른 사서 자주 사용하는 것이 이익이 되므로 빨리 살 것을 촉구하는 의미이다.

2   Purchasing

Expressions

회원이지 않아?

'회원이야?'는 어떤 사람이 회원인지 여부

를 몰라서 물어볼 때 쓰지만, '회원이지 않아?'는 회원이라는 사실을 알고 있는 상태에서 확인하고 싶을 때 쓴다. 'N이지 않아?'는 자신이 알고 있는 것에 대한 확신을 가진 상태로 상대방에게 그 사실을 다시 가볍게 확인할 때 사용하는 표현이다.

VIP 등급일걸?

'VIP 등급일걸?'은 확실하지는 않지만 VIP 등급이라고 추측할 때 쓰는 표현이다. 'A/V을걸?'은 추측에 대한 확신이 비교적 강하지만 단정적인 느낌을 피하고자 사용하며 끝을 올려서 말해야 한다.

주문해 주면 안 돼?

이는 '주문해 줘'와 비슷하게 어떤 것을 주문해 달라고 부탁할 때 사용하는 표현으로, 'V아/어 주면 안 돼?'를 사용해서 부탁하면 명령형인 'V아/어 줘'보다 간절하고 부드러운 느낌을 준다.

- - - - - - - - - - - - - - - - - - -

3   Making an Inquiry

재입고 될까요?
가능한지도 궁금하네요.
포장해 주시나요?

'A/V을까요?', 'A/V은/는지 궁금하다', 'A/V나요/은가요?'는 문의할 때 자주 사용되는 종결 어미로 친절하고 예의 있는 느낌을 준다. 'A/V은/는지 궁금하다'는 완곡하게 말하는 느낌이며 'A/V나요/은가요?'는 부드러운 느낌이다.

고기가 상할까 봐 걱정됩니다.

이는 고기가 상할 수 있는 경우가 생길지도 몰라서 걱정하고 있다는 뜻이다. 혹시라도 생길 가능성이 있는 나쁜 일에 대해 걱정할 때 'A/V을까 봐 걱정되다'를 사용한다.

배송해 주시는 거 맞죠?

'A/V은/는 거 맞죠?'는 자신의 요청 사항을 상대방에게 한 번 더 상기시킬 때나 자신이 알고 있는 사실을 확인할 때 사용한다.

- - - - - - - - - - - - - - - - - - -

4   Issues and Returning

나도 됐다.

'됐다'는 권유 받았을 때 거절하는 표현으로, 다정하거나 상냥한 느낌은 아니고 단정적인 느낌을 준다. 따라서 가깝고 편한 사이에서 주로 사용되며 예의 있게 거절하려면 '괜찮아요, 아니에요' 등으로 부드럽게 표현하는 것이 좋다.

환불 받고 싶은데 어떻게 하면 돼요?

'어떻게 하면 돼요?'는 방법, 절차 등을 몰라서 안내 받고 싶을 때 사용하는 표현이다. 앞부분에 'A/V은/는데'를 사용해서 자신의 상황을 설명할 수 있다.

죄송해서 어쩌죠?

'죄송해서 어쩌죠?'는 너무 미안해서 어쩔 줄 모르는 감정을 친근하게 나타낼 때 쓸 수 있는 표현이다. 비슷한 표현으로 '죄송해서 어떡하죠?'가 있다.

저희 측

'측'은 다른 쪽과 상대하여서라는 의미로 대화와 관련된 당사자들 중에서 어느 한 쪽 그룹을 가리킬 때 사용한다. 저희 측은 우리 측의 겸양어로 주어로 사용할 때는 'N이/가 대신', 'N에서'를 함께 쓴다.

4. 오늘은 하루 종일 넷플릭스
Today, I'm Watching Netflix All Day Long

1 Selecting Content

Expressions

[비] **집콕**

'집콕'은 '집에만 콕 박혀 있다'를 줄인 신조어로 집에서 나오지 않고 틀어박혀 있다는 뜻이다. '집콕, 집콕하다'의 형태로 쓸 수 있다. 비슷한 표현으로 방에만 콕 박혀 있다는 의미인 '방콕하다'도 있다.

볼 만한 거 뭐 있어?

'V을 만한 거 뭐 있어?'는 어떤 것을 추천해 달라는 뜻으로, 무난하면서 괜찮은 수준의 것을 추천 받고 싶을 때 사용하는 표현이다.

에이, 뭐야?

이는 기대했던 것에 대해 실망하거나, 황당한 일에 어이없는 감정을 나타내는 표현이다. 억양에 따라서 놀람, 감동, 짜증 등의 다양한 감정을 나타낼 수 있다.

2 Watching Content

Dialogue

Tips

남주: '남자 주인공'의 줄임말. 여자 주인공은 여주

Expressions

남주가 뭐래? / 뭐라는 거야?

남자 주인공의 대사를 알아듣지 못해서 같이 보던 사람에게 뭐라고 했는지 물어볼 때 '남주가 뭐래? / 뭐라는 거야?'라고 한다. 주변 소음, 말하는 사람의 발음이나 목소리 크기, 말하는 속도 때문에 무슨 말을 했는지 잘 듣지 못했을 때, 그 장소에 같이 있던 다른 사람에게 발화 내용을 묻기 위해 사용한다. 하지만 억양에 따라 짜증이 섞여 있는 느낌을 줄 수 있으므로 주의해야 한다.

못 알아듣겠어.

이는 들어도 그 뜻을 이해할 수 없다는 의미이다. '못'과 '겠어'가 함께 사용되어, 하려고 애써도 할 수 없다는 뜻으로 1인칭 화자의 발화로만 사용할 수 있다.

아무래도 자막 켜고 보는 게 낫겠다.

이는 잘 안 들려서 앞으로 다시 돌려 보기도 하고 소리를 키워 보기도 했으나, 효과가 없으니 결론적으로 자막을 켜고 보는 게 좋겠다는 의미이다. '아무래도'는 이리저리 생각해 보거나 이것저것 해 봐도라는 의미이며, '아무래도 V는 게 낫겠다'는 표현은 고민하

고 이것저것 시도한 후, 결론을 내리고 앞으로 어떻게 할지 나타낼 때 사용한다. 'V는 게 낫겠지?'의 형태로 동의를 구하기도 한다.

3 Evaluating Content

Dialogue

Tips

(미쳤)음: -음은 동사나 형용사와 결합하여 명사형을 만들어 주는 기능을 하는 어미로, 최근에는 리뷰, 카톡 대화, 인스타그램 게시물 등 온라인 상에서 한 두 문장의 짧은 글을 남길 때 주로 사용된다.

Expressions

[유] **제발 이 드라마 안 본 사람들 없게 해 주세요.**

이는 이 드라마를 안 본 사람이 없었으면 좋겠다는 의미이다. '안 V아/어 본 사람들 없게 해 주세요'는 인터넷에서 어떤 것을 적극적으로 추천할 때 사용하는 표현으로 어떤 것이 너무 좋아서 모두가 경험해 봤으면 좋겠다고 바라는 의미를 담고 있다.

미쳤음

'미쳤다'는 최고이다, 정말 좋다, 뛰어나다라는 의미로 사용되는 신조어 표현이다. 일반적인 상황이 전혀 아니거나 보통의 사람은 할 수 없을 정도로 그 수준, 품질, 능력이 매우 뛰어나다는 의미를 담고 있다.

[유] **구멍이 없음**

이 표현에서 '구멍'은 허점, 약점, 부족한 점, 또는 그런 약점을 가진 사람이라는 뜻이며 '구멍이 없다'는 부족하거나 뒤쳐지는 부분이 하나도 없이 모든 것이 좋다는 의미이다. 개인뿐만 아니라 여러 명이 팀으로 작업하는 드라마, 영화, 아이돌 그룹, 스포츠 팀 등에 대해서 평가할 때 사용한다.

[비] **역대급**

'역대급'은 대대로 이어 내려온 그동안을 뜻하는 '역대'와 등급을 뜻하는 '급'이 합쳐진 신조어이다. 문법상으로는 맞지 않는 표현이나, 지금까지 없었던 최고의라는 의미로 일상생활, 신문, 방송 등에서 자주 쓰이고 있다. '역대급이다', '역대급으로' 등의 형태로 사용된다.

4 Canceling and Reasons

Expressions

일단 해지했다가 그때 봐서 재가입하자.

이는 먼저 해지를 하고 나서 나중에 다시 가입하자는 뜻이다. 나중을 생각하지 않고 우선 어떤 행동을 한 다음에, 추후 상황을 보고 다음 행동을 할지 말지 결정하겠다는 뜻이다. 'V았/었다'가 앞뒤에는 서로 반대되는 행동을 나타내는 단어가 사용되어야 한다.

그거 얼마나 한다고?

'그거 얼마나 한다고?'는 그건 금액이 비싸지 않으니까 신경을 쓸 필요가 없다는 의미의 반문이다. 형태는 의문문이지만 의미는

평서문이므로 대답할 필요는 없다. 무시하는 느낌을 줄 수 있으므로 억양에 주의해야 한다.

귀찮긴 뭐가 귀찮아?
이는 상대방의 발화 내용을 강하게 부정하거나 동의하지 않을 때 비꼬듯이 사용하는 반문의 표현이다. 바로 직전 상대방의 발화에서 동의하지 않는 부분의 단어를 가져와서 표현에 사용해야 한다. 상대방이 무시당하는 느낌을 받을 수 있으므로 상대를 가려 주의해서 사용해야 한다.

5. 저녁에 뭐 시켜 먹지
What Should We Order for Dinner?

1 Using the Delivery App

Expressions

밥 하기 귀찮은데 배달시켜 먹을까?
이는 배달시켜 먹자고 제안할 때 사용하는 표현으로, 'A/V은/는데'를 이용하여 그 이유와 상황을 설명할 수 있다.

[비] **매운 음식이 좀 땡겨.**
'땡기다'는 비표준어로, 원칙적으로 '당기다'가 알맞은 표현이다. 특정 음식이 먹고 싶어질 때 사용할 수 있다. '매운 음식이 당겨'와 같이 사용되는 것이 맞으나 '매운 음식이 땡겨'로 쓰는 경우가 훨씬 많다.

얼마 안 걸려.
'얼마'가 부정을 나타내는 '안'과 함께 사용될 때는, 구체적인 수치를 밝히지 않고 수량, 값, 정도가 적다는 것을 강조하는 표현이 된다. '얼마 안 걸리다'는 짧은 시간임을, '얼마 안 하다'는 적은 돈임을 나타내고, '얼마 안 되다'는 시간, 돈, 거리 등 다양하게 쓰인다.

2 Confirming and Serving Delivery Food

Expressions

먹을 만큼만 덜어서 먹자.
'V(으)ㄹ만큼만'은 필요 이상으로 지나치게 많지도 않고 부족하지도 않게 딱 필요한 정도를 나타내는 표현으로, '먹을 만큼만 덜어서 먹자'는 적당한 양만 덜어서 먹자는 의미이다.

덜어서 먹자.
'덜어서 먹다'는 어떤 양을 덜고, '그' 덜어낸 것을 먹는다는 뜻으로 'V아/어서'는 연속성에 놓여 있는 동작을 연결할 때 쓰는 표현이다.

오래 걸려서 그런지 음식이 좀 식어서 왔어.
음식이 식어서 온 이유를 시간이 오래 걸렸기 때문이라고 추측을 하긴 하나, 확실하게 단정할 수 없어서 '오래 걸려서 그런지'라고 표현했다. 'A/V아/어서 그런지'는 이유를 추측하는 표현이며, 그것이 뒤에 나타나는 결과의 이유나 원인일 것 같지만 확실하게 판단할 수 없을 때 쓸 수 있다.

먹으면 되지, 뭐.

간단한 해결책을 제시할 때 'A/V으면 돼'로 표현할 수 있다. 하지만 그 해결책이 완전히 마음에 들지는 않아서 아쉬움이 느껴지긴 하나, 그걸 선택해도 크게 문제가 되지 않을 때는 'A/V으면 되지'라는 표현을 쓴다.

- -

3 Eating Food

배 터질 것 같아.

'터지다'는 둘러싸여 막혀 있던 것이 뚫리거나 찢어진다는 뜻으로 '풍선이 터지다', '폭탄이 터지다'와 같이 쓰인다. 무언가를 많이 먹고 배가 가득 차서 더 이상 먹을 수 없을 때 풍선이 터지는 것처럼 '배가 터질 것 같다'고 표현한다.

[비/유] **국룰**

'국룰'은 '국민의 룰'을 줄인 신조어로, '국룰'의 '룰'은 영어 rule을 한국어로 표기한 것이다. 하지만 이는 강제적인 규정을 뜻하는 게 아니라 많은 사람들 사이에서 당연하게 행해지는 보편적인 행위를 유머스럽게 표현한 것이다. 'N은/는 국룰이다'라는 형태로 주로 사용된다.

[유] **볶음밥은 못 참지.**

'참다'는 감정이나 생리적인 현상을 억누르고 견딘다는 뜻을 가지고 있어, '눈물을 참

다, 화를 참다' 등으로 사용된다. 그러나 'N은/는 못 참지'라고 굳어진 표현은 유행어가 되어 참을 수 없을 정도로 너무 좋아서 꼭 해야 한다는 의미를 가진다.

나중에 한입만 달라고 해도 안 준다.

'한입'은 한 번에 먹을 만한 음식물의 양을 나타내는 말로, 주로 가족이나 친구 등 친한 사이에서 상대방이 뭔가를 먹고 있을 때, 맛있어 보여 맛보고 싶으면 '한입만 (줘), 한입만 먹을게'라고 말한다.

음식을 만들거나 주문할 때는 자기는 먹지 않겠다고 하다가 음식을 보면 막상 마음이 달라져 같이 나눠 먹자고 하는 사람도 있다. 음식이 나와도 그 사람에게 음식을 절대 나눠 주지 않겠다는 의미로 음식을 준비할 때 '나중에 한입만 달라고 해도 안 줄 거야'라고 얘기한다.

- -

4 Leaving Reviews

Expressions

평점이 높은 데는 이유가 다 있네요.

'이유가 다 있다'는 어떤 사건이나 결과에는 그 이유가 반드시 있다는 뜻이다. 특히 그 결과를 누구나 다 수긍할 수 있을 때 'A/V은/는 데는 이유가 다 있다'라고 표현하며 'A/V은/는 데' 앞에는 이유가 아닌 결과를 써야 한다. '평점이 높은 데는 이유가 다 있네요'는 왜 평점이 높은지 수긍할 수 있다는 의미를 가지고 있다.

비/유 **찐맛집**

'찐'은 '진짜'에서 '진'을 강하게 발음한 것으로 최고, 아주 좋은, 거짓이 아닌의 뜻을 가진 접두사가 되었다. '찐맛집'은 '찐'과 '맛집'이 결합된 신조어로, SNS등의 홍보로 유명해진 식당이 아닌 진짜 음식이 맛있는 식당이라는 의미다. '찐'은 'N이/가 찐이다', '찐으로' 등으로 활용되기도 한다.

비/유 **가성비**

'가격 대비 성능의 비율'의 줄임말로 정해진 가격에 비해 성능이나 품질, 효율의 정도를 의미하는 신조어이다. 주로 '가성비가 좋다', '가성비가 훌륭하다', '가성비 맛집', '가성비가 별로다' 등으로 사용된다.

6. 우리 만날래?
Want to Meet Up?

----

1 Deciding on a Place via KakaoTalk

Vocabulary

카카오톡

'카카오톡'은 한국의 대표적인 메신저 앱으로 '카카오톡'을 줄여서 '카톡' 혹은 '톡', 여러 명이 참여하는 채팅방을 '단톡방(단체 톡방)'이라고 한다. 거의 모든 국민이 이 앱을 이용하는데 대학이나 직장 등에서 '카톡'의 '단톡방' 기능을 이용하여 공지를 하거나 회의를 진행하고, 심지어 공공기관에서도 일반인을 대상으로 고지서를 '카톡'으로 전달하기도 한다. '카톡'은 공적인 기능뿐만 아니라 사적인 친목 모임에도 많이 이용된다. 자주 어울리는 친구들이나 가족들 사이에 '단톡방'이 있으며 이를 통해 사진이나 정보를 공유한다. 특히 모임 약속을 정할 때 '투표하기' 기능을 통해 모임 시간이나 장소를 정하게 되고, 모임에서 쓴 돈을 '정산하기' 기능을 통해 손쉽게 똑같이 나눠서 낼 수 있다.

Expressions

비/유 **ㅇㅇ**

메신저 앱에서 간단한 답을 쓸 때 상대방도 의미를 충분히 짐작할 수 있는 경우에는 전체 단어를 입력하는 대신 초성만 쓰기도 한다. '감사합니다'는 "ㄱㅅ", '수고하세요'는 "ㅅㄱ", '오케이'는 "ㅇㅋ", '응'은 "ㅇㅇ"으로 짧게 써서 효율성을 높인다.

비/유 **핫한 삼겹살 집**

이는 인기가 많은 삼겹살 식당이라는 의미이다. '핫하다'는 영어 hot과 '하다'가 결합된 표현으로 최근 인기를 많이 끌고 있는 것에 두루 쓰인다. 인기 있는 장소라는 뜻으로 '핫플레이스 hot place'의 줄임말인 '핫플'도 흔히 쓰이고 있다.

비/유/속 **읽씹**

'카카오톡'에서는 상대방이 메시지를 읽었는지의 여부를 확인할 수 있는데, 상대가 메시지를 확인했음에도 불구하고 답을 하지 않을 때 '읽씹'이라는 표현을 쓴다. '읽씹'은 '읽고 씹다'의 줄임말로 '씹다'는 무시하다라는 의미를 가지는 비속어이므로 사용에 주의가 필요하다.

2 Reserving and Notifying

Expressions

비 **맞는 듯.**
'맞는 듯'은 '맞는 듯하다'의 줄임말로 맞는 것 같다라는 의미이다. 원래는 문어체로 일상 대화에서는 잘 쓰지 않지만, 메신저 앱에서는 효율적으로 쓰기 위해 줄여서 자주 사용한다.

비/유/속 **빡세.**
'빡세다'는 하는 일이 아주 어렵고 힘들다는 뜻을 가진 사투리이다. 요즘은 전국에서 다 사용되고 있지만 속된 느낌이 나므로 사용에는 주의가 필요하다.

헷갈리지 말고 잘 찾아와.
명령형의 문장에서 부정의 'V지 말고'를 사용해서 한 번 당부하고, 명령이나 부탁을 또 한 번 함으로써 이중으로 당부하면서 그 뜻을 더 강조한다.

3 At a Restaurant

Vocabulary

Tips

벨
한국에서는 식당에서 종업원을 부를 때 '저기요'와 같은 표현으로 말할 수도 있지만, 규모가 큰 식당에는 그 소리가 잘 닿지 않기 때문에 테이블마다 종업원을 부를 수 있는 차임벨이 있다.

진동벨
카페 등에서 주문한 것이 나오면 종업원이 큰 소리로 부를 수도 있지만, 규모가 큰 곳에서는 그 소리가 잘 닿지 않기 때문에 주문할 때 종업원이 진동벨을 준다. 진동벨이 울리면 진동벨을 가지고 픽업 장소로 가서 주문한 것을 받으면 된다.

Expressions

유 **진실의 미간**
'미간'은 양 눈썹 사이를 말하는데 일반적으로 감정적인 동요가 있을 때 미간을 찡그리게 되므로 찡그린 미간을 거짓 없이 솔직한 반응으로 생각한다. 특히 맛있는 음식을 먹었을 때 그 맛에 감탄하며 자기도 모르게 미간을 찡그리게 되는 경우가 많아서 그것을 '진실의 미간'이라고 부른다. '진실의 미간이 나오다' 등으로 사용된다.

그렇게 맛있어?
상대방이 맛있게 먹는 모습을 보며 그런 표

정이나 행동이 나올 정도로 맛있냐고 물어볼 때 '그렇게 맛있어?'라고 한다. 상대방의 감정이나 느낌이 표정이나 행동으로 나타날 때 그 정도로 강렬한지 약간은 신기해하면서 물어보는 표현이다.

(더) 달라고 할까?

이는 식당에서 추가 주문하기 위해 동행자와 논의할 때 쓰는 표현이다. '[(더) 주세요]라고 할까?'를 간접 화법으로 바꾼 것으로 '(더) 달라고 할까?'는 하나의 표현으로 굳어져 흔히 쓰이고 있다.

비 셀프

'셀프 서비스'는 영어 단어 self-service를 한글로 표기한 것으로 이를 줄여 '셀프'라고 하기도 한다. 식당에서 '물은 셀프입니다'라는 안내문을 흔히 볼 수 있는데, '물은 손님이 직접 가져다 드세요'라는 뜻이다. 뿐만 아니라 한국에서는 반찬들이 무료로 제공되기도 하는데 식당 한 켠에 직접 가져다 먹을 수 있도록 마련된 반찬 코너가 있다. 보통 물, 반찬, 개인 접시 등이 '셀프 서비스'가 많다.

---

4 Paying and Settling Up

Expressions

얼마 나왔어?

식당에서 먹은 총 금액을 확인할 때 '얼마야?'도 쓰지만 더 흔히 쓰는 표현이 바로 '얼마 나왔어?'이다. 그에 대한 대답도 '3만 원이야'보다 '3만 원 나왔어'라고 하는 것이 더 자연스럽다.

비/속 N빵

'N빵'이란 여러 명이 모여 같이 식사를 하거나 선물을 준비할 때, 전체 금액을 인원수대로 나누어 부담하는 것을 말한다. 그 인원수를 N이라고 쓰는 이유는 수학에서 미지의 수, 정해지지 않은 수를 나타낼 N을 쓰기 때문인데 인원수가 정해져 있는 상황에서도 'N빵' 혹은 '1/N'이라고 표기하고 '엔빵', '엔분의 일'이라고 읽는다. 자신이 먹은 것을 각자 계산하는 방식이 아니라, 식당에서 한 사람이 카드로 결제하고 나서 나중에 계좌이체나 '카카오톡'의 정산하기 기능 등을 통해서 그 사람에게 돈을 보내면 된다.

1차

한국의 모임은 일반적으로 집이 아닌 외부 공간에서 이루어진다. 일단 식당에서 식사를 먼저 하고, 자리를 옮겨 카페를 가거나 술집을 가게 되는데, 이렇게 자리를 옮길 때마다 '1차, 2차, 3차' 등으로 표현한다.

---

7. 행복해지고 싶다면 떠나라
If You Want to Be Happier, Leave

---

1 Before Reaching the Destination

Expressions

돌아가면서 운전하면 되잖아.

이는 한 명이 계속해서 운전하는 게 아니라 다른 사람들도 순번을 정해 차례를 옮기며 운전하는 것이다. '돌아가면서'는 어떤 일을 혼자 계속하는 것이 아니라 여러 명이 번갈아 가며 한다는 뜻이다.

이왕 가는 거 우리 가고 싶은 데 다 가자.

'이왕'은 일이 이미 정해졌으니라는 의미를 가지고 있고, 그 상황에서 할 수 있는 것들 중에 최선의 선택을 하는 것이 좋다는 의미의 표현이 그 다음에 나와야 한다. 이때 '이왕 V는 거'의 형태로 주로 사용된다.

총무

'총무'란 기관이나 단체에서 전체적이며 일반적인 사무를 맡아보는 부서나 사람을 뜻한다. 여기에서 유래되어 일반 친목 모임에서도 '총무'는 모임에서 주로 연락을 담당하고 모임 회비 등을 관리한다. 여행에서의 '총무'는 호텔, 식당, 카페 등에서 한꺼번에 계산을 하고 나중에 정산까지 담당하는 역할을 하게 된다. '총무를 하다', '총무를 맡다' 등으로 쓰인다

---

2   At the Accommodation

Expressions

이제 막

'이제 막'은 말하고 있는 바로 지금을 뜻하는 표현으로, 어떤 일이 일어난 지 얼마 안 된 짧은 시간임을 강조한다.

[비/유] 뷰 맛집

'맛집'은 음식이 맛있는 식당을 뜻하지만, 거기에서 확장되어 식당뿐만 아니라 뭔가를

잘하는 곳, 뭔가가 좋은 곳을 뜻할 때도 쓰이게 되었다. '뷰 맛집'은 뷰가 좋은 곳의 의미를 가지고 있다.

아침에는 어떨지 완전 기대돼요.

확실히 알 수는 없지만 어떤 좋은 일이 생기길 바라며 기다리게 되는 것을 나타낼 때, 의문사와 결합하여 'A/V을지 기대되다'라는 표현을 쓴다.

---

3   At a Must-Eat Place

Expressions

[유] 실화

'실화'는 지어낸 이야기나 소설이 아닌 실제로 있는 이야기를 뜻하는 말이다. 최근에는 여기에서 의미가 확장되어 어떤 사실을 직접 보거나 들었지만 믿을 수 없을 정도로 놀랐을 때, 이것이 거짓이 아닌 진짜가 맞는지 확인하는 물음으로 쓰인다. 주로 '이거 실화냐?', '이거 실화임?'의 형태로 주로 사용된다.

일정이 다 꼬이는데 어떡하냐?

'어떡하냐'는 '어떻게 하냐'의 줄임말로, 문제가 생겨서 어떻게 하면 좋을지 논의를 시작할 때나 단순히 걱정이나 염려를 나타낼 때 쓸 수 있는 표현이다. '어떡해?', '어떡하지?' 등으로 사용된다. 'A/V은/는데'로 연결하여 문제 상황을 설명한다.

[유] 이건 좀 아니지.

어떤 상황이나 일이 올바르지 않거나 마음

에 들지 않아 않아서, 그 일에 반발하며 현
상황의 문제점을 짚고 싶을 때 '이건 좀 아
니다'라고 한다. 구체적인 항의 내용에 '이건
좀 아니지', '이건 좀 아닌 것 같아', '이건 좀
아니지 않아?'라는 표현을 덧붙여 그 내용
을 강조할 수 있다.

---

4 Taking and Sharing Photos

Expressions

비 **인증 샷**
'인증 샷'은 '인증'과 영어 shot을 한국어로
표기한 '샷'이 결합된 말로, 어떤 행위를 한
것을 증명하거나 자랑하기 위해 남기는 사
진을 뜻하는 말이다. 주로 자신의 SNS에 올
리는 것으로 마무리된다. '샷'은 다른 단어와
결합하여 다양하게 사용된다.

딱
'딱'은 빈틈없이 정확하게 맞다는 뜻을 가진
부사로 'N이/가 딱이다'라는 형태로 주로 쓰
여 '100% 잘 맞다, 좋다'의 의미를 가지게
되었다.

좀 그렇다.
'N이가 좀 그렇다'는 별로 마음에 들지 않을
때나 의견에 반대할 때 쓰는 표현이다. 그러
나 그 이유를 구체적으로 밝히지 않고 말함
으로써 부정이나 거절을 보다 부드럽게 나
타낼 수 있다.

Index

ㄹ

ㅇ

ㅍ

ㅎ

ETC